CURTISS TRIAD (U.S.) 1911

AVRO BIPLANE (BR.) 1911

VICKERS FE-6 (BR.) 1913

MORANE-SAULNIER TYPE "L" (FR.) 1913

DEPERDUSSIN (FR.) 1913

SOPWITH TABLOID (BR.) 1913

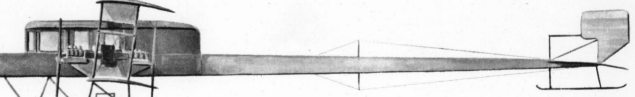

SIKORSKY GRAND (RUSSIA) 1913

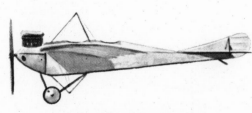

RUMPLER TAUBE (GER.) 1913

CURTISS AMERICA (U.S.) 1913

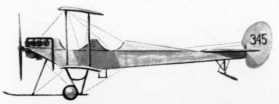

FARNBOROUGH BE-2 (BR.) 1913

MARTIN "TT" (U.S.) 1914

From The American Heritage
History of Flight

By the Editors of AMERICAN HERITAGE,
The Magazine of History

Editor in Charge
ALVIN M. JOSEPHY, JR.

Narrative by
ARTHUR GORDON

With two chapters by
MARVIN W. McFARLAND

The History of Flight

ADAPTED FOR YOUNG READERS BY SAREL EIMERL

 GOLDEN PRESS · NEW YORK

PICTURE CREDITS

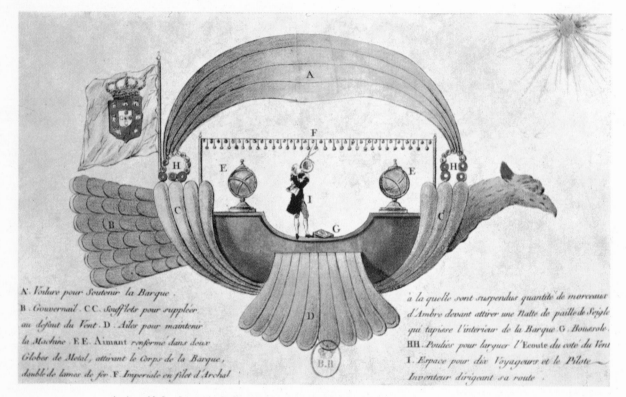

X. *Voilure pour Soutenir la Barque.*
B. *Gouvernail.* C.C. *Soufflets pour suppléer au défaut du Vent.* D. *Ailes pour maintenir la Machine.* E.E. *Aimant renfermé dans deux Globes de Metal, attirant le Corps de la Barque, double de lames de fer.* F. *Imperiale en filet d'Archal*

à la quelle sont suspendus quantité de morceaux d'Ambre devant attirer une Natte de paille de Seigle qui tapisse l'interieur de la Barque. G. *Boussole.* HH. *Poulies pour larguer l'Ecoute du coté du Vent.* I. *Espace pour dix Voyageurs et le Pilote Inventeur dirigeant sa route.*

A fanciful picture of Gusmao's "great bird." The picture is inaccurate and the model may actually have flown successfully as an unmanned glider.

ON THE COVER: *B-47 Stratojet.*

TITLE PAGE: *Orville Wright aboard and Wilbur Wright running alongside, as the first powered, man-carrying airplane rises into the air, December 17, 1903.*

Library of Congress Catalog Card Number: 64-20400

CONTENTS

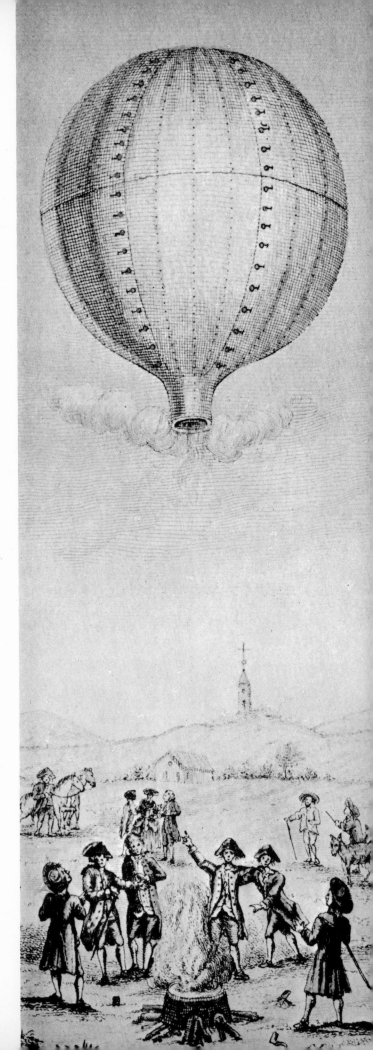

A contemporary French print of the Montgolfier brothers' first balloon.

CHAPTER ONE

Eagles were said to have carried the throne of the legendary Persian flying king, Kai Kawus.

The Wonder of Wings

FOR thousands of years, man looked up into the skies and dreamed of flying. Probably it was the birds which put the idea of flight into his mind. Century after century, he watched the easy acrobatics of the birds with amazement and admiration, and wondered how they came to possess such a marvelous gift.

Because they could not fly themselves, many men came to regard the power of flight as a form of magic. Some primitive peoples invented imaginary creatures, such as demons and dragons, angels and devils, who possessed the mysterious secret of flight. Other peoples made up stories about flying carpets and chariots, aerial boats, and other imaginary ways to soar through the air.

Usually, the ability to fly was looked on as a sign of strength and power. Most primitive peoples invented imaginary beings whom they worshipped as gods; and because wings were a sign of power, many of these gods were supposed to possess them. Even the Greeks and the Romans, who were far from primitive, gave wings to some of their gods. The Greek god Hermes was supposed to carry his messages through the skies with the aid of winged sandals; and Eros, the Greek god of love, was portrayed as a winged child.

Men also made up legends about people who had learned to fly. One of the earliest of such legends was invented by the Chinese. About four thousand years ago, according to the story, when the Emperor Shun was a boy, his father ordered him to go to the top of a tall granary. He then set the granary on fire. But Shun escaped by seizing two wide-brimmed hats and using them as a parachute to float safely to the ground.

The Chinese invented many other legends about flight. Lei Kung, their ancient god of thunder and lightning, was supposed to have the wings of a bat. And a man named Ki-kung-shi was said to have invented a flying chariot nearly four thousand years ago.

Nearly all early civilizations had similar legends about flying gods and heroes. Kai Kawus, an ancient king of Persia, was said to have traveled on a flying throne drawn by four hungry eagles. They carried it through the air by frantically flapping their wings as they tried to reach slabs of meat suspended just beyond their reach.

The best known of all flying legends is the Greek story of Daedalus and Icarus. It tells how Daedalus and his son, Icarus, were trapped inside the labyrinth of King Minos, ruler of Crete. In order to escape, Daedalus built two sets of wings made of feathers which were bound together with wax. He gave one set of wings to Icarus and instructed him to keep a middle course. "If you fly too low," he warned, "the waves will wet the feathers and make them too heavy for flight. If you fly too high, the heat of the sun will melt the wax and the wings will fall apart." But Icarus was too bold. Higher

Demigods scatter flower petals on dancers in this eighteenth century A. D. *Indian painting.*

and higher he flew until, just as Daedalus had warned him, the sun's rays melted the wax that bound his feathers, and he plunged to his death in the sea.

These are just stories. But even in distant times, people were experimenting with flight. More than two thousand years ago, the Chinese had learned how to build kites, and some people believe that during the Middle Ages they constructed monster kites which were big enough to lift men.

The most obvious way for a man to attempt flight was to jump from a high place, wearing some kind of artificial wings which might support him in the air. Probably there were many men who risked their lives in such attempts. One of them was a Saracen who, in the eleventh century, climbed to the top of a tower in Constantinople and threw himself off the edge. He wore a long white garment, stiffened with willow poles, which was supposed to help him to glide. But his body was too heavy for the willow poles to support, and he fell—instead of gliding—to the ground.

About five hundred years later, an Italian adventurer named John Damian also tried to glide, this time off a castle wall. Damian's wings were made of chicken feathers. They, too, failed to support him and he plummeted to the ground.

As far as we know, the first man to come up with any practical ideas about flying machines was the Italian Leonardo da Vinci, who was born in 1452. Leonardo was one of the most brilliant men who have ever lived. He was a great painter and architect; he was also a musician, a mathematician, and a physicist. He was passionately interested in flying and he foresaw many developments which did not actually take place until several hundred years after his death. For example, he drew up designs for a pyramid-shaped parachute and for a model helicopter.

Another sketch by Leonardo, the first man to design a parachute.

In Leonardo's time, there were no engines capable of driving a full-size flying machine. Even if there had been, Leonardo was on the wrong track in one very important way. Taking his ideas from the birds, he believed that man should use some kind of flapping mechanism, similar to a bird's wings, to support him in the air. But this belief that man could copy the birds was a mistake, for a man's body is so different from a bird's that it cannot be held aloft by flapping wings.

Another Italian, named Giovanni Danti, who lived at the same time as Leonardo, is believed to have tried to fly, as Leonardo suggested, with the aid of flapping wings. He may have made some faltering glides over a lake about the year 1490. But his attempts to fly came to an end, according to one story, when his left wing gave way as he was trying to glide from a tower, and he was badly injured.

Almost two hundred years later, a French locksmith named Besnier claimed that he had actually flown, as the birds do, by sheer muscle power. He is supposed to have used two light rods which he balanced on his shoulders. He attached one end of the rods to his ankles with cords, and held the other end in his hands. Each rod was equipped with cloth panels hinged so that they closed on the upstroke and opened on the downstroke.

A spring-driven helicopter was only one of Leonardo's many ideas for possible flying machines.

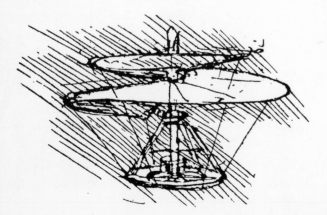

10

Besnier claimed that he kept jumping from higher and higher places until finally he flew over a barn. But few people believed him and one Italian scientist, G. A. Borelli, wrote a book proving that man's pectoral muscles were too weak for him to imitate the birds.

About sixty years after Borelli wrote his book, a French nobleman, the Marquis de Bacqueville, made yet another attempt to copy the birds. He announced that he was going to fly across the River Seine. With some kind of wings attached to his body, he leaped from the roof of his riverside mansion. Of course, his attempt was a failure and he came crashing down onto a washerwoman's barge, breaking his leg as he landed.

Most people, however, agreed with Borelli that man could not fly by imitating birds. For about a hundred years after he wrote his book, the hope of heavier-than-air flight was practically abandoned. But there was another possibility. Perhaps man could achieve flight in a machine that would be carried upwards because it was lighter than the surrounding air.

Actually, one vital clue to the possibilities of lighter-than-air flight had been staring man in the face for thousands of years. This clue existed in the smoke that drifted upwards from a fire. Obviously, if man could somehow find a way to make use of the force that drove smoke and sparks upwards he might be able to build a machine that would fly.

One such attempt may have been made, soon after 1700, by a priest named Laurenço de Gusmão. He tried to achieve flight with both heavier-than-air and lighter-than-air machines. The heavier-than-air device displayed a rather advanced design for its day. Many people made fun of Gusmão's machine, but it is possible that he managed to fly it as a glider, without a man aboard.

Gusmão's lighter-than-air device was a miniature hot-air balloon. According to one account, the balloon "rose to a small height against the wall and then came to earth and caught fire when the materials became jumbled together. In descending and falling downwards, it set fire to some hangings and everything against which it knocked."

The accident was unimportant. If the story of his balloon is true, Gusmão's achievement was to

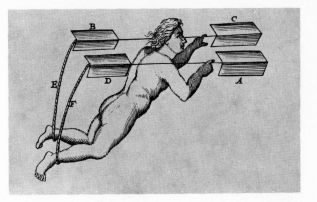

The machine which Besnier claimed to have flown by using the muscular power of his arms and legs.

realize that air rises when it is heated. If this heated air could be kept in a suitable container, it could presumably be used to carry that container—and perhaps additional weights, such as men—up into the sky.

Some years later, an English chemist named Henry Cavendish made another extremely important discovery. He found that hydrogen—then known as "inflammable air"—was much lighter than ordinary air. Apparently, Cavendish did not realize that his discovery might lead to flight. But Joseph Black, a chemistry professor at Glasgow University in Scotland, instantly spotted the significance of Cavendish's discovery: that a very light container filled with hydrogen would be lighter than air and would therefore rise. Black thought that his students would be interested to see such an experiment, and he set about finding a substance light enough to act as a container. But by the time such a container had been prepared, he had moved on to another part of his course. He never performed the experiment.

Another scientist, Tiberius Cavallo, heard of Black's planned experiment and decided to perform it himself. But none of the containers he tried was light enough and, finally, he gave up the hunt. He had come as close to inventing the balloon as anyone could without actually doing it.

As it happened, it was not Cavendish's discovery which led to the first balloon (or the second, if Gusmão actually did construct one). For the man who did, beyond any doubt, finally construct a balloon got his inspiration from the ancient clues of smoke and sparks.

CHAPTER TWO

The first free ascent in a hot air balloon was made in this gorgeously decorated vessel.

Ballooning

ONE winter's night in the year 1782, a French papermaker named Joseph Montgolfier was sitting in front of his fireplace. Joseph was interested in science and especially in the possibilities of flight. As he gazed into the fire, he suddenly realized that some gas or other force was lifting the smoke and the sparks.

That observation gave Joseph Montgolfier the idea of capturing the gas—or whatever it was that made the smoke rise—and using it to lift objects into the sky. He carried out his first experiment with an oblong bag, made of fine silk, which had an opening in the bottom. The experiment was simple; Joseph merely burned paper beneath the opening. Swelling into an awkwardly shaped sphere, the bag rose to the ceiling.

Joseph now realized that he had made a discovery which might prove tremendously important. Excitedly, he wrote to his brother, Etienne, who was also interested in science: "Prepare promptly a supply of taffeta and ropes, and you will see one of the most astonishing things in the world!"

Together with his brother, Joseph Montgolfier repeated his experiment, but this time he performed it out of doors. Inflated by hot air, the bag rose to about seventy feet.

The Montgolfier brothers next made two larger balloons, which they called "aerostatic machines." Both balloons rose with enough force to break the cords that held them down, and the second one soared to a height of more than a thousand feet.

The brothers used a fire made of chopped wool and straw. It produced great amounts of smoke, and the Montgolfiers decided that this smoke must contain some hitherto unknown gas which made the balloons rise. It never occurred to them that hot air alone could exert an upward pressure.

By the early summer of 1783, the brothers were ready to give a public demonstration. On June 4, they lit a fire under a balloon in the market place of the little town of Annonay. The balloon was a paper-lined linen bag with a circumference of more than a hundred feet.

The spectators were amazed to see that as the balloon filled with heated air it needed eight strong men to hold it down. At last Joseph gave the signal and the balloon was released. It soared to a height of about six thousand feet and landed more than a mile away.

The news of this event excited the members of the Academy of Sciences in Paris. They promptly invited the Montgolfiers to come to the capital and display their new machine. They also encouraged a young French physicist named J. A. C. Charles to carry out further research.

Charles remembered the "inflammable air" (hydrogen) which Henry Cavendish had discovered, and he decided to use it, instead of heated air, for his experiment. He knew that hydrogen would leak out through either paper or linen. So he asked two brothers named Robert to make him a container of silk fabric coated with rubber.

Charles ordered them to make a small "flying globe" about thirteen feet in diameter. The balloon was supposed to be ready for trial on August 23, 1783. But Charles had trouble accumulating enough hydrogen to keep the balloon filled, and it was not ready until the 26th.

Meanwhile, people had been growing more and more excited. The balloon was moved before dawn to avoid the crowds. But great numbers of spectators turned out anyway. Carrying torches to illuminate the darkness, they escorted the balloon through the Paris streets in a triumphant parade.

All next day, a crowd of more than fifty thousand people waited eagerly while Charles struggled to inflate his bag of silk. At last, at five in the afternoon, the balloon was released. By that time rain had begun to fall and the balloon rose into low-hanging clouds.

Benjamin Franklin was standing among the spectators. "Interesting," one spectator remarked to him as the balloon vanished from sight, "but what use is it?" The wise Franklin had immediately realized that this balloon was merely the first step toward flight. "What use is a newborn baby?" was his reply.

Charles' balloon came to a sad end. It floated down to earth outside Paris among country people who did not know what it was, and they attacked it with pitchforks. When the hydrogen came gushing out, they were frightened. So they tied the remnants of the balloon to the tail of a horse which dragged it to shreds on the country roads.

Meanwhile Etienne Montgolfier had come to Paris and was constructing a handsomely decorated aerostat, seventy-four feet high. He demonstrated it so successfully that he was invited to repeat the exhibition in front of King Louis XVI and Queen Marie Antoinette.

Etienne's balloon had been damaged by rain, but in four days he built another one. Both he and his brother were eager to know if living creatures could stay alive up in the air. So they attached a cage to the balloon, with a sheep, a rooster and a duck inside it.

With a fire burning underneath it to heat the air, the balloon rose into the sky, soared for eight minutes, and then drifted down to land a mile and a half away. The King was so delighted by this performance that he ordered a gold medal to be made, bearing the Montgolfiers' profiles and the words: "For having made the air navigable."

Hydrogen-filled balloons soon came to be known as *charlières,* after their inventor, Charles, and hot-air balloons became known as *montgolfières.* The two brothers were full of confidence after their success in front of the King, and they set to work constructing a balloon able to carry aloft a fire and a two-man crew to stoke it. These men would be risking their lives, and the King wanted to pick out two condemned criminals to make the ascent. If they landed safely, they would be allowed to live as the reward for their flight.

A huge crowd gathered to watch Madame Thible, the first woman who dared go up in a balloon.

13

Many people, however, felt that being the first men to fly was an honor not to be wasted on criminals. They managed to persuade the King to change his mind, and finally a young and enthusiastic doctor, Jean-François Pilâtre de Rozier, was chosen to make the ascent.

In October, 1783, Pilâtre made several trial ascents in balloons that were kept tied to the ground so that they would not float free. Then, on November 21, Pilâtre made the first real flight in an unsecured balloon.

He went up with the Marquis d'Arlandes, an infantry major. A wicker platform was attached to the straining montgolfière, and the two men stationed themselves on opposite sides of it. At fifty-four minutes past one o'clock, the balloon rose majestically into the air while the two men on the platform waved their hats triumphantly at the watching crowds below. Their journey lasted twenty-five minutes, and took them five miles across Paris.

At one point in the flight, sparks from the fire scorched holes in the balloon and threatened to burn the ropes holding the platform. The Marquis d'Arlandes doused the sparks with a wet sponge. "We were now," he wrote later, "close to the ground, between two mills. As soon as we came near the earth I raised myself over the gallery, and leaning there with my two hands, I felt the balloon pressing softly against my head. I pushed it back, and leaped down to the ground. Looking round...I saw [Rozier] in his shirt sleeves creeping out from under the mass of canvas that had fallen over him . . . we were at last all right." For the first time in history, man had moved freely through the air.

Ten days later, Professor Charles made his first flight in a hydrogen-filled balloon, taking one of the Robert brothers with him as a passenger. The charlière was a big one, with enough room to carry food, extra clothing, scientific instruments, and even some bags of sand for ballast.

While 200,000 Parisians watched, Charles and his passenger rose into the air from the Tuileries Gardens in Paris. Their voyage was a tremendous success. In the first two hours, the balloon sailed to Nesle, about twenty-seven miles from Paris. There Robert got out. Charles decided to make

Waving flags, Charles and Robert leave the Tuileries in the first hydrogen balloon ascent.

another ascent on his own. With only one passenger aboard, the balloon rose rapidly to a height of nine thousand feet. But Charles was troubled by the cold and by a pain in his ear brought on by the change in air pressure, and he soon came back down, making an expert landing.

These balloon flights created tremendous excitement, and ballooning became a craze. Soon, pictures of montgolfières and charlières began to appear as decorations on plates and vases. But for quite a while, only a few daring spirits actually ventured up into the air.

A handsome young Italian, Vincent Lunardi, who was working in London, was one of the most famous of the early balloonists. He made his flight in a balloon carrying also a dog, a cat, a pigeon, a bottle of wine, and some food. According to Lunardi, his voyage had the effect of saving someone's life. At one point along his route, a jury was trying to decide whether a criminal was guilty or not guilty. When they heard of Lunardi's approach, the members of the jury were so anxious to see the balloon that they instantly reached a verdict of "not guilty," so that they could watch Lunardi sail past.

That summer a Madame Thible became the first woman to go up in a balloon. She made her ascent in a montgolfière, and during the trip she sang a song from a comic opera: "Oh, to travel in the clouds." The following summer, an English lady, Mrs. Sage, also went up in a balloon. She and her companion landed in a field and greatly annoyed a farmer by trampling his beans.

This incident was comical. But it did illustrate a serious difficulty. The balloonists could not control their direction. Some of them tried to steer with oars or paddles or revolving fans which were crude ancestors of propellers. But these hand-operated instruments could do little to counter the force of the wind on the balloon.

The first man to come up with an effective answer to the problem was a young French lieutenant of engineers, Jean-Baptiste Meusnier. He realized that the best way to make a steerable balloon (or dirigible, as it was called) was to give it an elongated, sausage-like shape: thin at the bow and stern, and fat in the middle, like a ship.

In 1785, Meusnier produced a design for a dirigible. The section which contained the gas was to have an elongated shape, like a football. Slung below it, there was to be a car powered by three propellers and steered by a rudder in the form of a sail. The propellers were to be worked by man power.

Meusnier even sketched a hangar which would house his dirigible and a portable canvas shelter to cover it in the open. But, unluckily, he never built his dirigible. Nine years after he designed it, he was killed in battle.

Meusnier's ideas were far ahead of his time. Dirigibles were not built for nearly another hundred years. But, in 1785, two men did succeed in crossing the English Channel in a balloon.

The pilot, a Frenchman named Jean-Pierre Blanchard, had been interested in flying for many years. He claimed that he had been experimenting with parachutes as early as 1777. In 1781, he designed and built a "flying chariot" with four beating wings like those of a bird. This machine never flew. But when the first charlière made its successful flight, Blanchard turned to balloons and soon made successful ascents in both England and France.

These flights attracted the attention of an American-born doctor, John Jeffries, who lived in England. Jeffries was tremendously interested in ballooning and eager to go on the first flight across the Channel. He even offered to get out at any time during the crossing—in other words, to jump to his death—if it became necessary to lighten the balloon.

Blanchard, apparently reluctant to share the honor of making the first Channel crossing, did everything he could to discourage Jeffries. At one point, he secretly weighted himself with lead to make himself heavier and show that the balloon could not carry more than one person. But Dr. Jeffries discovered the trick and a quarrel broke out which had to be settled by the governor of Dover Castle.

Meusnier's brilliant design for an elliptical airship which, unfortunately, was never built.

At last, on January 7, 1785, the balloon took off from Dover with both men aboard. Blanchard had some aerial oars and a propeller which had to be worked by hand. The balloon also carried thirty pounds of sand for ballast, two anchors, two cork life jackets in case of a forced landing in the sea, brandy, some food, and a large parcel of pamphlets to be scattered over France.

At first all went well. The wind was favorable and the balloon sailed serenely over ships in the Channel which saluted by dipping their colors. But when the balloon reached two thousand feet, it became necessary to release some of the hydrogen. In the process, the balloon lost too much gas and went into a terrifying series of ups and downs.

Trying to level the balloon by making it lighter, Blanchard and Jeffries began to dump ballast desperately. First they threw the sand overboard, then the pamphlets, then everything else that was movable except the life jackets. They unscrewed the propeller and threw that out. Next they tossed the two anchors overboard and finally they began to cast off their outer garments.

At last, as it neared the French coast, the balloon was light enough to rise slowly. Then, shivering in the January cold, Blanchard and Jeffries found that the balloon was plunging down again, this time into a forest. They tossed out their life jackets, which were now useless. Still, the balloon continued to drop and reached the tops of the trees. But the two men managed to stay aloft until they came to an open space. There, they opened a valve and the balloon, losing air, sank to the ground about twelve miles inland from Calais.

In both England and France, Blanchard and Jeffries were greeted as heroes—and indeed they were. Blanchard made many more flights in Europe. He was the first man to go up in a balloon in Holland, Germany, Belgium, Switzerland, Poland, and Czechoslovakia. He traveled to the United States and on January 9, 1793, he made the first aerial ascent in America. He carried a flag decorated on one side with the Stars and Stripes and on the other with the French Tricolor.

Fourteen months after the first balloon ascent, Blanchard and Jeffries cross the Channel.

Pilâtre de Rozier, the first man to go up in a balloon, was impressed by the praise showered on Blanchard and Jeffries. Perhaps he was also a little envious. Whatever the reason, he decided to copy their Channel crossing, going this time from France to England.

Blanchard's balloon had almost come down into the water through loss of hydrogen. To avoid this risk, Pilâtre decided to use both hydrogen and hot air. In other words, he intended to combine the hot-air montgolfière and the hydrogen charlière. The airship was to consist of a spherical charlière, filled with hydrogen, with a cylindrical montgolfière underneath.

Pilâtre's idea was that by controlling the heat of the fire he would be able to control the lift of the balloon. But his plan was extraordinarily dangerous. It was known that hydrogen would explode if fire got to it, and Professor Charles himself warned Pilâtre that he was trying to mix fire and gunpowder.

Pilâtre remained determined to go through with the flight, but he was not optimistic about his chances of success. He told friends that he was "certain of meeting with death," and he swore that if he did reach England, he would never again go up in a balloon.

Despite the risks, two Frenchmen competed furiously for the chance to go with Pilâtre. One was Pierre Romain, who had constructed the balloon. The other was a young aristocrat, the Marquis de Maisonfort. He was so anxious to make the trip that he offered to pay a large sum of money just for a place. But Pilâtre objected so vehemently to having two other men aboard that the Marquis finally gave up.

Early on the morning of June 15, 1785, the balloon took off from Boulogne with Pilâtre and Romain aboard. The wind had appeared to be favorable, but though the balloon rose to three thousand feet within half an hour, it did not make much progress toward England.

People watching from the ground could see that Pilâtre and Romain were doing something to the fire basket that swung below the montgolfière.

In this giant striped balloon, the Nassau, *Charles Green flew a record-breaking 480 miles.*

Then a blue flame appeared, a muffled explosion was heard, and the car came hurtling down, trailing smoke and shreds of silk. Both Pilâtre and Romain were killed.

This tragedy was the beginning of the end of hot-air ballooning. Some people continued to fly montgolfières, especially for the purpose of getting up into the air so they could make parachute jumps. But confidence in the hot-air method was badly shaken.

Other balloon enthusiasts experimented with new ideas. One of the greatest was the Englishman Charles Green, who made his first ascent in 1821. Green's great contribution to ballooning was a guide rope, long enough to hang from the balloon and trail along the ground.

As the balloon rose, more of the rope hung through the air and so served as extra ballast. As the balloon descended, more of the rope trailed on the ground, and thus the amount of ballast was reduced. The guide rope also had another purpose. At night, when the balloonist could not see, the feel of the rope acted as a warning, telling him when he was coming to higher ground.

In November, 1836, Green took off from London, accompanied by two passengers. The three men flew all night over France and Belgium, and landed the next day in Germany. They had traveled a record 480 miles. Encouraged by this success, Green began to talk of crossing the Atlantic by balloon. However, he never made the attempt. Instead he concentrated on shorter flights and by the time he retired at the age of sixty-seven, he had made five hundred ascents.

An American balloonist, John Wise, also had dreams of crossing the Atlantic. To prove that a west-to-east trans-Atlantic flight was possible, Wise and three companions set out from St. Louis on July 1, 1859. In nineteen hours, they flew 804 miles before their balloon came down in New York State. The 804 miles they covered was little more than a quarter of the distance across the Atlantic, but it remained a distance record for half a century.

Disaster strikes Wise and his companions as their balloon crashes after an 804-mile flight.

The crash did not end Wise's dreams of crossing the Atlantic. He was still trying to set endurance records at the age of 71 when he disappeared in a flight over Lake Michigan. But his greatest contribution to ballooning was not his record-breaking flight: it was his invention of the ripping panel. This was a special section of the balloon which balloonists could rip open when they landed to deflate the gas bag immediately, and so avoid the danger of being dragged all over the countryside.

But the balloonists' main problem was still unsolved. Balloons had enabled men to ascend into the sky but they were still completely unreliable because they could not be controlled and went wherever the wind took them. Both Meusnier, the French officer, and M.-J. Brisson, a French physicist, had suggested building balloons with elongated shapes back in the 1780's. The trouble was that no one could think of an effective way to power balloons and so make them independent of the wind.

All kinds of plans were suggested. Some people thought balloons could be propelled with oars. Others even suggested that airships should be harnessed to birds. One designer suggested in 1835 that eagles would make the best engines "if they could be tamed. But perhaps," he added, "strong pigeons would do."

These ideas were, of course, hopelessly impractical. One of the first advances toward powering a balloon was made by an Irishman, Monck Mason, who had accompanied Green on his flight from London to Germany. Mason constructed a model dirigible, forty-four feet long, which was powered by a clockwork-driven propeller. He exhibited this model in London, where it traveled short distances at speeds up to six miles per hour.

Nine years later, a French engineer, Henri Giffard, made an important advance. He slung a small, three-horsepower steam engine under an elongated balloon and hooked the engine to a huge, three-bladed propeller. This was the first real dirigible big enough to carry a man, and Giffard covered seventeen miles in it at a speed of five miles per hour.

In the next three decades, other designers tried to power dirigibles with coal-gas engines and

The gondola of one of Thaddeus Lowe's balloons rising above Union tents during the Civil War.

electric motors. But though these dirigibles flew, they were not really successful. For both electric motors and steam engines were too heavy for effective flight.

Even non-powered balloons, however, proved that they could be of practical use. Way back in 1783, when he watched Charles' first ascent into the air, Benjamin Franklin had realized that balloons might be valuable in war. John Wise reached the same conclusion. In 1846, when the United States was at war with Mexico, he suggested that a captive balloon be placed over the Mexican fort at Vera Cruz so that it could drop bombs on the garrison.

The U. S. War Department did not follow up this idea and it was the Austrians who finally carried out the first air assault in history. In 1849, when besieging Venice, they sent small hot-air balloons over the city. Each one carried a thirty-pound bomb with a time fuse.

Andrée's balloon started well (above) but its journey was ended by the weight of ice (below) five hundred miles from the North Pole.

Balloons played an important role in the Franco-Prussian War, when the Germans invaded France and besieged Paris. Throughout the four-month siege, the French used balloons to maintain contact between the besieged capital and the provinces. They carried 2,500,000 letters and more than a hundred persons, including the leader of the French government, out of the city. Sixty-six balloons were built and flown out of the city; six were captured by the Germans and two were lost at sea.

Balloons were also proving that they had their uses in peacetime. In 1867 Henri Giffard had dis-

played a captive balloon at a fair in Paris. It was a tremendous success and thousands of spectators bought tickets to enjoy the exhilarating experience of rising high into the air.

Giffard's example was soon followed elsewhere, and going up in a balloon became one of the main attractions at fairs and carnivals in Europe and the United States. The balloonists themselves also developed special acts to thrill the crowds. Year by year, they rose higher and stayed in the air longer, and the more daring ones performed stunts such as descending to the ground by a parachute fired from a cannon.

This was all good fun. But ballooning also had its tragedies. One of the worst occurred in 1897 when three men tried to reach the North Pole in a balloon and never returned.

The flight was the idea of a Swedish engineer named Salomon Andrée. He had a balloon built in France which could retain its gas for thirty days, and on July 11, 1897, he and two companions set out on their flight from Spitsbergen across the Arctic Ocean. They carried sails and trailing guide ropes, navigating devices which, they hoped, would enable them to follow a direct course to the Pole.

In the first two days of the flight, the balloonists sent back two messages. One was carried by a carrier pigeon; the other was placed in a buoy. After that there was silence.

Thirty-three years were to pass before the outside world learned the fate of Andrée and his companions. On August 6, 1930, a group of Norwegian explorers came across a silent Arctic camp, three hundred miles east of Andrée's starting point. There they found the bodies of the three men, together with some undeveloped films and a diary which Andrée had kept.

The diary told the story of what had happened. As the balloon proceeded toward the Pole, ice began to form on it, and after three days it became so heavy that it was forced down, finally coming to a halt four hundred miles from Spitsbergen but five hundred miles from the Pole.

Andrée and his companions first set up camp at the place where the balloon came to rest. But at last, faced with starvation, they set off to try and find help. For two and a half months, they struggled across the ice, occasionally shooting animals to provide food. But finally, having walked as far as they could, they set up their last camp. And there, huddled together for warmth, one by one they died.

Meanwhile, other balloonists were carrying on the search for an effective way to power a balloon, and so transform it into a true dirigible. The first big step toward a workable solution came in 1885 when a German, Karl Benz, built the first practical gasoline-powered automobile. Living in Paris there was a rich Brazilian named Alberto Santos-Dumont, who became an early automobile enthusiast. He was also interested in flying, and in 1898 he decided to see if one of the sputtering motorcar engines could be used to power a balloon.

Santos-Dumont had a lot of bad luck. One airship collapsed while landing. A second rammed into trees and was damaged. A third was broken up and destroyed by a group of ruffians. The wind created by the propeller of yet another dirigible gave Santos-Dumont pneumonia. But in the end he achieved success and went on to build a dozen small, powered airships which became a common sight over Paris.

Santos-Dumont's dirigibles were little more than toys. But he had pointed the way to much larger and more useful ones. On November 13, 1902, a 190-foot airship, called the *Lebaudy,* made its

Alberto Santos-Dumont just before an ascent

first ascent at Moisson, France. The following May it traveled 23 miles, and in November, 1903, it flew the 38½ miles from Moisson to Paris. These voyages were made at speeds of up to 26 and 28 miles per hour and were the first long-distance flights by a powered airship.

It was well over a hundred years since the Montgolfier brothers' balloons had first risen into the air. The process of producing a steerable balloon had been a long one. But the balloonists had finally proved that properly powered airships could cover long distances at a fair speed and go wherever the men in control wanted them to.

The Lebaudy, *a motor-driven tapered dirigible, demonstrated the possibility of powered flight.*

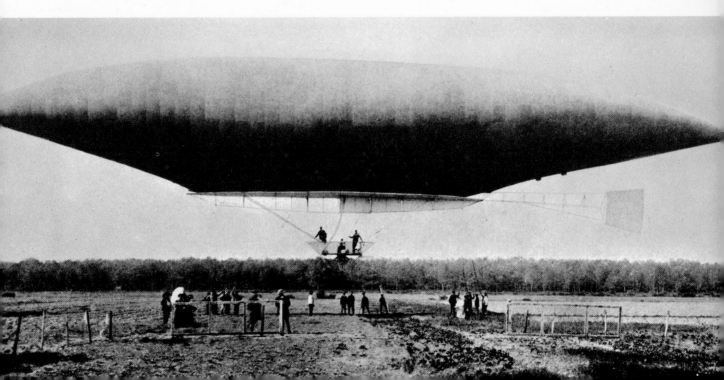

An imaginative view of the Ariel, designed by W. S. Henson, shows his dream of a flying steam carriage. But the weight of an engine made it impossible for such a machine to leave the ground.

CHAPTER THREE

Sir George Cayley

Learning to Fly

THROUGHOUT the 1800's, the balloonists searched for ways to steer and control their balloons. Meanwhile another group of inventors were approaching the problem of flight from a different angle. They believed that man's best chance to fly lay in a heavier-than-air machine supported by wings.

The first man to make important progress toward a flying machine with wings was an Englishman named George Cayley. In 1783, when he was nine years old, Cayley was thrilled by news of the Montgolfier brothers' flight. In his excitement, he began to experiment with paper balloons and lighted candles. Gradually his experiments became more advanced. In 1804 he built a device with a whirling arm which stirred up the air like a propeller. With this device, Cayley was able to study the effects of air pressure on a plane surface set at various angles.

Later still, experimenting with gliders, Cayley made two very important discoveries. He found that if wings were set to form a shallow V, they gave the glider lateral stability, that is, they kept it from tipping from side to side. He also found

23

that a tail plane set behind the main wings was needed to keep a glider from tipping forwards or backwards. The tail plane provided what is called longitudinal stability.

Cayley flew his first glider in 1804. He attached a diamond-shaped kite to a light pole, to form a kind of wing, and added a tail with vertical and horizontal fins, or stabilizers. The glider was only a model with a wing area of 154 square inches, but it was a great step forward. Cayley sailed it down a steep hill and remarked that it looked "very pretty." Actually this glider was, in many ways, the first airplane device ever built.

Cayley's 1804 sketch for a fixed-wing glider

Cayley then went on to build bigger gliders. In 1849 one of them lifted a ten-year-old boy off the ground for several yards while sailing down a hill. According to a story told by his granddaughter, Cayley had an even bigger success in 1853. He persuaded his coachman to make a trial run in a glider that lifted him across a shallow valley and set him down in a cloud of dust. "Please, Sir George," the outraged coachman is supposed to have shouted, "I wish to give notice. I was hired to drive, and not to fly!"

Cayley's gliders were not proper airplanes, of course, because they did not have an engine to power them. They could only sail downhill or be

Cayley's 1849 triplane. Floating downhill, it carried a ten-year-old boy for several yards.

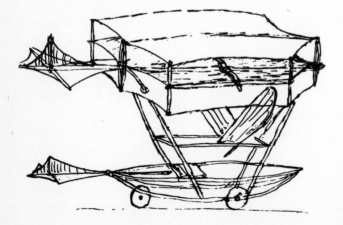

carried along by a strong wind. Cayley himself was keenly aware that his gliders were only a preliminary step toward controlled flight. "The whole problem," he wrote in 1809, "is confined within these limits, *viz.*—to make a surface support a given weight by the application of power to the resistance of air."

Cayley had already grasped the basic principle which governs flight in a heavier-than-air machine. The air flowing over the top of a wing travels faster than the air flowing underneath it. This means that the air presses harder against the bottom of the wing, giving it lift, or upward push. The faster the air travels, the less there is on top of the wing. So the plane which moves fastest obtains the most lift.

Obviously an effective machine needed to have an engine to drive it forward and stir up enough resistance in the air to keep it aloft. But in Cayley's day, the only effective engines were those driven by steam, and they were much too heavy to be used in flying machines.

But not all the inventors realized this. Another Englishman, William Samuel Henson, had grown up in the age of steam. He watched the first public railroad come into existence in England and he had seen the first steam-powered ships that crossed the Atlantic. He therefore assumed that steam could also be used to power a flying machine.

In 1842, Henson patented his plan for what he called an "Aerial Steam Carriage." The design made use of many of Cayley's ideas. The airplane had a single wing with a span of 150 feet, a tail plane shaped rather like a bird's tail, a vertical rudder, and a three-wheel landing gear. It was to be powered by a steam engine enclosed in the fuselage below the wing, and this engine was to drive two propellers.

The power-driven propeller was Henson's great contribution to the development of airplanes. A propeller is shaped so that the air flows faster over the front of the blade than over the back. The pressure is therefore less at the front than at the back and the propeller is driven forward, carrying the plane with it. The propeller can be placed in front of the wing; then it pulls the plane through the air. Or, it can be placed behind the wing and will push instead of pull.

Henson's design was the first reasonable and detailed plan for a powered airplane. But it would never have flown; the weight of the steam engine alone would have made flight impossible. In 1847, Henson and his friend John Stringfellow built and tested a model of the Aerial Steam Carriage with a twenty-foot wingspan. Even with the engine working, it was only able to glide downwards, and Henson gave up in disgust.

Stringfellow carried on alone. In the following year, he built a smaller model based on Henson's design. It had a tiny steam engine driving two four-bladed propellers and was launched from a cradle suspended on a wire. It managed only a kind of part-powered, part-glide flight. Stringfellow now realized that a steam engine could only be used successfully on small models and he gave up his experiments for the next twenty years.

At this point, French inventors took over the lead. In 1857, a naval commander named Felix Du Temple patented a design for a powered airplane that was more advanced in many ways than Stringfellow's model. Its wings were set in a shallow V to keep it from tipping sideways, and it had a propeller set at the front of the fuselage to pull it through the air. Before building a full-size machine, Du Temple tested a scale model which rose into the air under its own power—the first fixed-wing machine ever to do so. Actually the propeller stopped in mid-air, but the wings acted as a parachute and kept the plane level until it settled back onto the ground on its wheels.

By 1874, Du Temple had his full-size machine ready, powered by a hot-air engine. No one is quite sure what happened to this machine. According to one report, it took off down an inclined ramp and made a short hop into the air, with a young sailor aboard. If this story is true, Du Temple's machine was the first to ascend, or hop, into the air under its own power while carrying a man.

Alphonse Pénaud added several important innovations. Pénaud first experimented with model airplanes powered by elastic bands. These bands were twisted tight before the plane was launched; once in the air, the plane's propeller was turned by the force of the elastic unwinding. Pénaud used his models to study the problems of balance in the air. He set the wings at a shallow V and

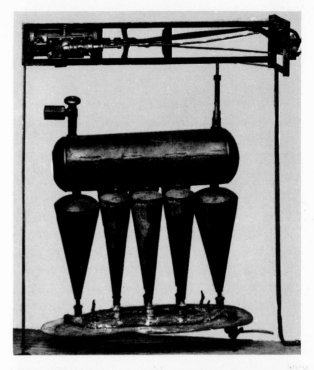

Stringfellow's steam engine provided power for the first powered flight of an unmanned flying machine.

this gave the models lateral stability. A tail assembly set some distance behind the main wings at a downward angle kept the models from tipping backwards or forwards. One little plane flew more than forty yards in eleven seconds.

In 1876, Pénaud patented a design for an amphibious airplane. It included the first joy stick, a steering column which controlled both the airplane's elevation and direction. It also included a retractable landing gear and a glass covering over the cockpit. Pénaud planned to power the plane

Pénaud's model, powered by twisted rubber bands

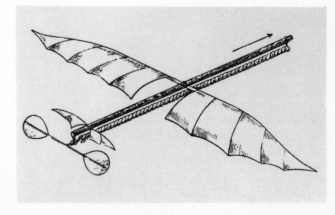

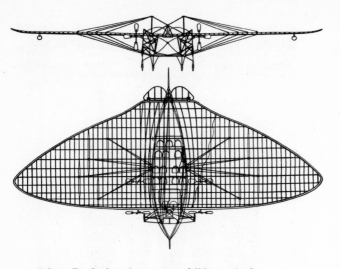

Pénaud's design for an amphibious airplane never built because there was no engine to power it.

with two propellers mounted in front but here he ran into the old problem: there was no suitable engine available. With his plans made useless by the lack of a proper engine, and discouraged and depressed by the ridicule pioneers must endure, Pénaud, at the age of thirty, put a bullet through his marvelous brain.

Most would-be fliers still believed that the lack of a lightweight engine was the main barrier to winged flight. They assumed that if they could somehow be boosted into the air, the actual control of the plane in flight would be easy. Toward the end of the 1800's, one of the world's best-known inventors set himself to develop an engine powerful enough to launch a plane into the air. He was Sir Hiram Maxim, an American-born inventor who had become a British subject. He had made himself rich and famous by inventing many things, notably a machine gun.

Maxim laid out a railroad track half a mile long on his estate in England. On it he built a giant flying machine. Its main wing was 110 feet long and four feet wide, and it was powered by two enormous steam-driven propellers which, at full throttle, could develop 360 horsepower.

Maxim was interested in measuring the amount of power needed to lift a machine off the ground; he was not really interested in flying. A few inches above the track he built a system of guard rails to hold his machine down in case it rose too high.

In 1894, Maxim drove his three-and-a-half-ton machine along the track. Gradually he increased the steam pressure until the machine began to rise. It broke through the guard rails, and Maxim, afraid of losing control, immediately shut off the steam. Slightly damaged, the machine came to a halt.

Maxim believed that he had removed the main barrier to successful flight. "Propulsion and lifting," he announced, "are solved problems; the rest is a mere matter of time." Actually, this was nonsense because powering a plane and lifting it off the ground was only one part of the problem of flight. Learning to control the plane once it was in the air was just as important and probably more difficult.

This control could only be learned through actual practice in the sky. One of the first men to carry out this essential practical research was a German, Otto Lilienthal. He did his research in gliders with a specific purpose in mind. He wanted to master the art of flying so that, when a suitable engine was finally developed, man would know exactly how to control an airplane in flight.

Lilienthal's first gliders were monoplanes with a slightly arched wing and a fixed tail plane. The pilot dangled like a marionette from the glider, with his head and shoulders above the wings and his body and legs below. He controlled the glider as best he could by shifting his weight and swinging his hips and legs forward and back or from side to side.

Lilienthal built a cone-shaped hill of earth so that he could take off downslope and into the wind, no matter which way it blew. In his heavy shoes and close-fitting cap, he looked like a mountain climber. Between 1891 and 1896 he made more than two thousand glides; some of them covered several hundred feet.

By 1896, Lilienthal was ready to attempt powered flight. He had built a glider with flapping wing tips and, to power it, he had built a small motor driven by compressed carbonic acid gas. But on August 9, he made what should have been a routine flight in one of his ordinary gliders. The weather was blustery and a gust of wind suddenly pitched his craft sharply upwards. The glider stalled and crashed to earth from about fifty feet, breaking Lilienthal's back. He died the next day.

Lilienthal was the first man to prove beyond any doubt that the air could support a man in winged flight. Photographs of him manipulating his gliders appeared in newspapers all over the world. They stirred up a tremendous interest in flying and many adventurous young men began to experiment with gliders.

But the man who took the next great step forward was already in his fifties when he became fascinated by the problem of flight. Samuel Pierpont Langley was a distinguished American astronomer and director of the Smithsonian Institution in Washington. In 1889, a little aero steam engine designed twenty years before by John Stringfellow was presented to the Smithsonian. Langley studied the historic engine, realized that better steam engines could be built, and decided that he could build them.

Langley called his airplanes "aerodromes." By 1891, he was ready to test a model aerodrome, but the frame was too heavy and the model would not fly. Langley was not discouraged. For the next five years he kept on doggedly building models which would develop enough power to fly but not be too heavy to stay aloft.

In 1896 he achieved a success, with a steam-powered double monoplane; it had two wings with one set in front of, instead of above, the other.

The model flew for three-quarters of a mile and came down only when the fuel gave out.

Langley did not at first win much credit for this achievement. Like other inventors, the men who experimented with these early flying machines were often ridiculed. Many people considered that manned flight was impossible and they jeered at Langley for wasting his time with such children's toys as model airplanes.

Langley's money, meanwhile, was running low and he seemed to have no chance of building a full-size airplane, one big enough to carry a man. But in 1898 he had what appeared at first to be a tremendous stroke of luck. The United States went to war with Spain and the War Department showed keen interest in a controllable, power-driven airplane that might be useful in war. The Congress therefore gave Langley $50,000 and told him to go ahead and build his machine.

Langley by now had become convinced that a gasoline engine would be more suitable than a steam engine. He went to one manufacturer after another, asking them to build an engine that

Lilienthal prepares to make one of the daring flights which aroused much interest in gliders.

would deliver twelve horsepower and weigh only one hundred pounds. But the manufacturers could not produce it and in the end Langley used an engine designed by a New York inventor named Stephen Balzer. It was one of the first radial engines, with the cylinders arranged around the crankshaft like spokes around the hub of a wheel.

The engine weighed 125 pounds, which was more than Langley had hoped for, but when tested it developed 53 horsepower, an enormous achievement for the time.

Langley used his favorite design for his "aerodrome." It was a double monoplane with a tail plane and vertical rudder behind. Before building the full-size airplane, Langley tested a quarter-size model. It was the first flying machine to be driven by a gasoline engine and its flight was a complete success.

By October, 1903, Langley was ready and confident that his "aerodrome" was about to make the first sustained, man-carrying, heavier-than-air flight in history. He decided to launch the plane from a catapult mounted on a houseboat in the Potomac River. At noon on October 7, the engine was started with Langley's assistant, Charles Manly, at the controls. The engine ran perfectly.

Samuel P. Langley and his pilot, Charles M. Manly

The twin propellers hurled back columns of air, and the 730-pound plane strained for release.

The next day a reporter for the *Washington Post* told the rest of the story: "A few yards from the houseboat," he wrote, "were the boats of the reporters. . . . The newspapermen waved their hands. Manly looked down and smiled. Then his face hardened as he braced himself for the flight, which might have in store for him fame or death. The propeller wheels, a foot from his head, whirred around him one thousand times to the minute. A man forward fired two skyrockets. There came an answering 'toot, toot' from the tugs. A mechanic stooped, cut the cable holding the catapult; there was a roaring, grinding noise—and the Langley airship tumbled over the edge of the houseboat and disappeared in the river, sixteen feet below. It simply slid into the water like a handful of mortar . . ."

Langley believed that some part of the machine had fouled the launching gear. His failure should have warned him to abandon his catapult altogether and to set his machine on wheels. But Langley decided to continue with the catapult. Ignoring all the jibes and the jeers, he salvaged his "aerodrome," repaired it, and on December 8, he tried again. Once again the catapult fouled the "aerodrome"; again it tumbled into the river, and again Manly was pulled out, dripping but unhurt.

Langley's second ignominious failure delighted the people who enjoyed ridiculing the early fliers. Throughout the country, newspapers were filled with a chorus of jeers about Langley and his flying machine. Langley was crushed and gave up his attempts to fly. But the jeers of his critics came at just the wrong time. For only nine days after Langley's second and final failure, a powered airplane ran along a track on a bleak North Carolina beach, sailed into the air, wavered along for twelve seconds, and then settled back into the sand. While the world was still laughing at Langley, the Wright brothers had flown.

The story of Wilbur and Orville Wright, the first men to conquer the air, is a straightforward tale of genius and tremendously hard work. They were the two youngest sons of a United Brethren bishop and they grew up in Dayton, Ohio. Early

in life, they were taught to be patient and methodical where any kind of effort was required. These were the qualities which, together with their natural genius, finally brought them success.

In later years Wilbur and Orville Wright agreed that they first became interested in flying when their father brought home a toy helicopter. Wilbur was eleven; Orville was seven. "A toy so delicate," they wrote, "lasted but a short time in the hands of small boys, but its memory was abiding."

As they grew older, the brothers began to experiment with toy helicopters they made themselves. When they became tired of toys, they started to fly kites. These kites were only a hobby, for the two young men had to earn a living. They worked together to produce a small newspaper; they worked for a while as printers. Finally they turned to manufacturing and repairing bicycles. It was a small business, but it provided them with enough money to pay for their experiments in aviation.

The Wright brothers realized that they had to solve three main problems in order to make a sustained flight. The first was how to shape an airplane's wings to provide enough lift. The second was how to maintain balance and control in the air. The third was how to apply power to a tested wing shape.

Like Lilienthal, the Wrights recognized that they could learn how to control a machine in the air only through constant practice. Wilbur compared flying to riding a horse. "Now, there are two ways," he said, "of learning how to ride a fractious horse: one is to get on him and learn by actual practice how each motion and trick may be best met; the other is to sit on a fence and watch the beast a while, and then retire to the house and at leisure figure out the best way of overcoming his jumps and kicks. The latter system is the safest; but the former, on the whole, turns out the larger proportion of good riders. It is very much the same in learning to ride a flying machine. . . . If you really wish to learn, you must mount a machine and become acquainted with its tricks by actual trial."

The Wrights were dissatisfied with earlier gliding techniques. Wilbur pointed out that a buzzard seemed to maintain its balance in the air chiefly by twisting its dropped wing. This twist increased the air pressure on the dropped wing and restored the bird to level flight.

The trick of wing twisting, or "warping," was one of the Wright brothers' two great techniques that led to greater control in the air. They attached strings to the wing tips of a box kite so that the wing tips could be warped. The strings could be operated from the ground.

The brothers' first glider was a biplane with a horizontal elevator flap in front and no tail unit.

29

The wing tips could be warped by means of cords operated by the pilot or from the ground.

The glider was shaped rather like a big kite and the brothers knew they would need a lot of wind to fly it. So they wrote to the Weather Bureau in Washington and were advised to try the beaches of North Carolina, where the winds swept in from the sea and there was plenty of open space.

In October, 1900, the brothers assembled their glider at Kitty Hawk, on the North Carolina coast. There they made a few glides in it, lying prone on the lower wing. "Our plan of operation," as Wilbur described it, "was for the aeronaut to lie down

A gay poster, advertising an 1898 musical, seems to promise an airship flying over New York City.

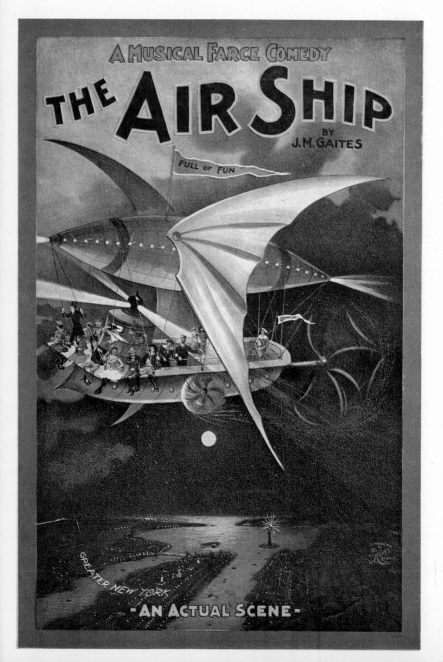

on the lower plane while two assistants grasped the ends of the machine and ran forward till the machine was supported in the air. . . . The man on the machine then brought the machine slowly to the ground. . . ."

The Wrights found that their glides were not dangerous, and although the glider sometimes landed at around thirty miles an hour, it was not damaged. But most of the time there was not enough wind to support a man on the glider and they had to fly it as a kite.

The following summer they came back to North Carolina, this time to Kill Devil Hills, four miles south of Kitty Hawk. To take more advantage of the wind, they had built a glider with greater curvature of the wings and a bigger wing area.

The Wrights' ideas about flying were very different from Langley's. He had wanted to build a machine which would be balanced automatically. In such a plane the pilot would have been simply a driver. The Wrights planned to build a machine which would be much more unstable but, at the same time, more "flyable." In their plane, the pilot's skill would be the main factor in control. He would keep the plane on an even keel by warping the wings, and he would keep it from tipping forwards or backwards by adjusting the elevator flap in front.

In the Wrights' second glider, the wires which controlled the wing warping were attached to the cradle in which the pilot lay. If he wanted to bank the plane to port (to the left), he swung his hips—and the cradle—to the left. This movement tightened the cable attached to the outer strut of the starboard (right) wing, and so pulled the rear edge of the wing downward. As the wing tip was pulled downward, the air pressure against it increased, pushing the wing upward and turning the plane to port.

At the same time, another cable attached to the cradle would give the port wing an up-warp. This movement reduced the air pressure on the port wing and pulled it downward. The simultaneous up-warp on one wing and down-warp on the other was an important feature of the Wrights' system.

Still the glider proved to have many faults and Wilbur Wright became depressed as the summer wore on. "Nobody will fly for a thousand years!" he said gloomily. The Wrights were learning how little they really knew about the principles of flight. That winter, when they returned to Dayton, they built a small wind tunnel, six feet long and sixteen inches square. Inside this tunnel they tested dozens of miniature wings and discovered what an English marine engineer named F. H. Wenham had learned forty years before: that most of the lift the wings provide comes from the front portion and that therefore a long, narrow wing provides more lift than a short, wide one.

The Wrights built this discovery into their third glider. They gave it wings that were less curved, longer, and not so wide. They kept the forward elevator but they also added fixed vertical fins in the rear.

When they tested this glider in September, 1902, it flew magnificently. In two months at Kitty Hawk the brothers made almost a thousand glides, some of them covering more than six hundred feet.

The glider had only one serious flaw. In a turn, the raised (down-warped) wing had to advance ahead of the other wing as the plane banked. But sometimes, when its wings were warped, the glider didn't turn. Instead of advancing, the raised wing would pull back and the machine would go sliding down into the sand with its dropped (up-warped) wing shooting out ahead.

It was Orville who finally found the explanation. The increased air pressure which caused a wing to rise also had the effect of slowing it down. Something had to be done to keep the machine turning and to turn it smoothly. The brothers therefore converted their fixed rear fins into a movable rudder and connected the rudder controls with the warping controls. The result was that, as the glider turned, the air pressure pushed the rudder forward and thus automatically counteracted the drag which had held back the down-warped wing.

Wing warping had been the Wrights' first great contribution to the technique of flying. Joining the warp and rudder controls was their second. By the time they returned to Dayton in October, 1902, the brothers had solved the main problems of controlling a plane in flight. By manipulating their forward elevator, they could rise or descend. With their wing warps and rudder controls working together, they could turn smoothly to right or left or restore horizontal balance. All they needed now was an engine to power their machine.

There was still no suitable lightweight gasoline engine in existence, so the Wrights decided to build their own. The engine they designed was water-cooled and driven by four cylinders. It weighed over two hundred pounds and developed twelve horsepower. The brothers were now sure that their calculations about power and weight were correct. They were confident that the engine would move their machine forward fast enough for the wings to lift it into the air.

Meanwhile the brothers had also been experimenting with new types of propellers, and they decided to use two propellers driven by a pair of long bicycle chains which were connected to the engine. As the propellers revolved, they produced a twisting effect liable to unbalance the plane. To counteract this force, which is called torque, the brothers made the propellers revolve in opposite directions.

In September, 1903, the Wrights crated up their machine and shipped it to Kitty Hawk. Various mechanical mishaps held them up until December, but at last they were ready. They arranged to launch their airplane off a light wooden rail about eight inches high. The plane was equipped with skids which fitted into the crossbeam of a little trolley that ran along the rail. A wire held the machine back until the engine was running at full throttle. Then the wire was released, allowing the plane and trolley to run smoothly down the track until—hopefully—the machine was airborne, leaving the trolley behind.

The brothers were ready by December 12, but they had to wait two more days for a sufficiently strong wind. They tossed a coin to decide who should make the first attempt, and Wilbur won. Few people had braved the chilly December wind to see the attempt and those who did come were quickly disappointed. The track had been laid down the slope of a dune to give the plane as speedy a take-off as possible. With Wilbur at the controls, the airplane went clattering down the track, rose too steeply, stalled, and fell back onto the sand.

Three days later, the Wrights tried again. This time the wind was so strong that they laid the track on a level stretch of sand. Again they hoisted the prearranged signal to alert the Life Saving Station down the beach, and five men came up to help them move the heavy machine from its hangar.

By now the wind was blowing more than twenty miles an hour, whipping the sand from the top of the dunes. It was Orville's turn to try and he fitted himself, face down, into the cradle on the lower wing. Slowly he brought the engine up to full power. The restraining wire was released and the trolley moved down the track, slowly at first and then faster, with Wilbur running alongside.

As he came to the end of the track, Orville raised the forward elevator and the machine rose. For twelve seconds it surged forward against the wind. Then it settled back onto the sand, 120 feet from the launching track. At 10:35 A.M. on December 17, 1903, for the first time, man had made a sustained flight in a heavier-than-air machine. The ancient dream of flying was a reality.

Orville described the historic flight in his diary in the methodical words of a scientist. "I found the control of the front rudder quite difficult," he wrote. "[It] had a tendency to turn itself when started so that the rudder was turned too far on one side and then too far on the other. As a result the machine would rise suddenly to about ten feet and then as suddenly, on turning the rudder, dart for the ground. A sudden dart when out about one hundred feet from the end of the tracks ended the flight. Time about 12 seconds. . . .''

That morning the brothers made three more flights. In the final one, Wilbur flew for fifty-nine seconds and covered 582 feet over land. But as the plane was bucking a stiff wind, it actually flew half a mile through the air. It was to be almost four years before anyone except the Wrights themselves equalled that distance.

After the last flight, a gust of wind caught the machine, turned it over, and severely damaged it. But the Wrights had won their triumph. Back in Dayton, their father received a telegram:

SUCCESS FOUR FLIGHTS THURSDAY MORNING ALL AGAINST TWENTY ONE MILE WIND STARTED FROM LEVEL WITH ENGINE POWER ALONE AVERAGE SPEED THROUGH AIR THIRTY ONE MILES LONGEST 57 SECONDS INFORM PRESS HOME CHRISTMAS OREVELLE WRIGHT

In those few words, which included a telegrapher's misspelling, Orville Wright summed up one of man's greatest scientific triumphs, a triumph that was to mark a turning point in human history.

Wilbur Wright (1867-1912)

Orville Wright (1871-1948)

CHAPTER FOUR

Ruth Oliver keeps pace with speeding racing car. Such races were popular in flying's early days.

Off We Go!

THE Wrights' sensational achievement did not at first create much of a stir. Newspaper editors were weary of claims that had proved false and of flying machines that did not fly. Most newspapers did not even mention the Wrights' success and the greatest aerial triumph of all time was greeted with general indifference.

The Wrights, however, were naturally anxious to show the world what they had accomplished. In the spring of 1904, they invited newspapermen to watch them fly a new, improved version of their flying machine. Unluckily, the wind was bad, the plane developed engine trouble, and the brothers could not even take off. Next day they tried again. But the engine failed on take-off and the machine abruptly halted. After that, the press completely lost interest.

Grimly, the brothers accepted the fact that they had much more work to do. They were off the ground, but only just. Their engine was so weak that they had to resort to the use of a catapult to help them take off. And their control of the plane in the air was still primitive and unreliable.

But by the following year—1905—the Wrights had developed another bigger and improved airplane. In it they could turn, bank, do figures of eight and stay aloft for astonishingly long periods. By the end of the summer, they were making flights that ended only when their fuel ran out. On October 5, for example, Wilbur flew for more than thirty-eight minutes and covered over twenty-four miles.

It was now almost two years since the Wrights' first successful flight and they were still the only people who had flown a powered machine with wings. But they had received neither fame nor encouragement. In January of 1905, they offered their invention to the United States War Department, but the Department rejected the offer without even bothering to inspect the brothers' machine.

The Wrights then decided to see if they could interest a European government in their invention. In 1907, they crated up one of their planes and took it to Europe. They were afraid that some competitor might steal their discoveries, so they refused to give a demonstration until they were paid $250,000. None of the European governments would pay so much money before they saw the plane fly, and so the brothers came home again, leaving their machine, still in its crate, in France.

Even before their trip, reports of the Wrights' work had begun to spread around Europe, especially in France. Back in 1903, an American engineer, Octave Chanute, who knew the Wrights, had visited France and described the brothers' 1902 glider in considerable detail, not omitting the key fact that the rudder and wing-warping controls were operated at the same time. By supplying these details Chanute gave French fliers a blueprint for success.

In order to encourage the French inventors, a rich French balloon enthusiast, Ernest Archdeacon, offered a prize to the first man who could fly twenty-five meters (about eighty feet). Alberto Santos-Dumont, who had built and flown twelve small dirigibles, heard of the prize. He built an airplane with box-kite wings set in a pronounced V. To keep the plane balanced, he put another box-kite far out at the front of the machine. It looked like a tailless goose with an outstretched neck, and Santos-Dumont flew it standing up.

On October 23, 1906, he managed to get his machine off the ground and fly nearly two hundred feet. Two weeks later, he flew 722 feet. These were the first heavier-than-air, powered, man-carrying flights made in Europe, and the continent was electrified by the news. For the Europeans simply did not believe that the Wrights had already conquered the air, and they hailed Santos-Dumont's flights as the first ever made.

Meanwhile, the Wrights were running into more trouble in America. They were facing competition from a lean, young, adventurous motorcycle racer named Glenn Curtiss. In addition to his racing, Curtiss had built lightweight engines for dirigibles which caught the attention of Alexander Graham Bell, the inventor of the telephone. Bell joined with Curtiss and others to form a research organization and they began to build airplanes which contained features copied from the Wrights and two French designers, Gabriel and Charles Voisin.

Their third plane, the *June Bug*, was a tremendous success. On July 4, 1908, with several hundred people watching, Curtiss flew it for more than a mile at Hammondsport, New York. This was the first wholly public flight in America and it won Curtiss a prize given by the magazine *Scientific American*.

The *June Bug* caused trouble between Curtiss and the Wrights. It was fitted with horizontal pieces, called ailerons, which were attached to the wing tips and could be moved up and down to produce the effect of wing warping. The Wrights believed that any kind of movable wing section was a copy of their own wing-warping invention, and they sued Curtiss for using their patented idea. The legal battle between them lasted for several years until the Wrights won.

But at last, in 1908, the Wrights finally achieved the fame they deserved. The change started in February when the United States Army accepted their bid to build an airplane for military use. The machine, said the Army, would have to be able to carry two men and enough fuel to go 125 miles, and it would have to fly at least ten miles nonstop at an average speed of forty miles per hour.

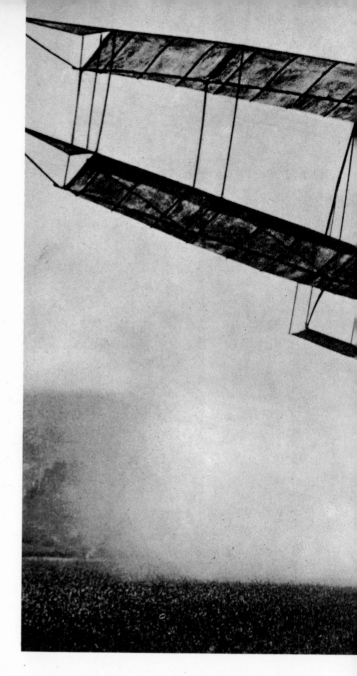

The next month, the brothers sold the right to build their planes in France for $100,000. Wilbur went again to France to demonstrate the machine which was still crated there, while Orville stayed at home to develop the machine ordered by the U. S. Army. However, the brothers had not flown for over two years, so first they went back to Kitty Hawk to regain their skill with their 1905 machine. They made one important change in it. They arranged to fly sitting up instead of lying down. Lying down minimized wind resistance but also caused painful cricks in the neck.

The French people and press still did not believe that Wilbur Wright could really fly. They soon learned they were mistaken. On August 8, 1908, he

took off from a racecourse near Le Mans. His machine slid easily down its track and up into the air, where it darted and soared about with the ease of a bird. At that time the French had only just managed to get their clumsy machines into the air. They were astonished by Wilbur's performance. "You should have seen the crowd there," an eyewitness reported. "They threw hats and everything. . . . Everyone was excited, and now, of course, the newspapers said what a marvelous man he was." Another member of the audience was an Englishman, Major B. F. S. Baden-Powell. "That Wilbur Wright," he prophesied, "is in possession of a power which controls the fate of nations is beyond dispute."

Glenn Curtiss won a prize for first flying his airplane, the June Bug, *a record 6,000 feet in 1908.*

Wilbur stayed on in France until the end of the year. He revolutionized European aviation, and the Europeans were delighted by his modesty, his good humor, and his willingness to share his knowledge and skill. One thing he did not like to do was make speeches. "I only know," he remarked, "of one bird, the parrot, that can talk, and it doesn't fly very high."

Meanwhile, Orville was having overwhelming success in the United States. On September 3, flying solo, he demonstrated his new two-seater at Fort Myer, Virginia. Effortlessly, he banked around the

parade ground while the spectators below went
wild with excitement. The government officials
were amazed by his performances. Day after day,
he continued to break his own endurance records.
But on the last day of the tests, a tragedy occurred. Orville was flying with a passenger, Lieutenant Thomas Selfridge, when a cracked propeller
produced a series of mechanical failures and the
plane crashed. Orville was badly injured and Lieu-

*Orville Wright circles the Ft. Myer parade ground
after making the first flight of over an hour.*

tenant Selfridge was killed, the first man to lose his
life in an airplane. But within ten months, Orville
was flying again and by the end of July, 1909, he
had finished demonstrating a plane that easily
satisfied the Army's requirements.

By this time, the new sport of aviation was
spreading fast. In 1909, the first flights were made
in Canada, Austria, Sweden, Rumania, Russia,
Turkey, and Portugal. J. T. C. Moore-Brabazon
became the first British subject to fly in Britain
and won a prize for making the first flight in an
English airplane.

Flying got another tremendous boost in 1909
from the first flight across the English Channel.
The *Daily Mail* of London had offered a prize of
a thousand pounds to the first man to fly the Channel, and an airman named Hubert Latham, who
was half-English and half-French, set out to capture it.

*Hubert Latham's attempt to fly the Channel
ended in failure a third of the way across.*

On July 19, 1909, Latham took off from France to cross the Channel. He was flying an Antoinette monoplane which had flap-type ailerons and a fifty-horsepower engine. When he was about a third of the way across, the engine failed and the plane went down. Luckily it floated nicely and Latham calmly smoked a cigarette as he waited to be picked up by a French destroyer that had been ordered to trail his plane.

Another Antoinette was made ready and Latham returned to his base in France to wait for favorable weather. Meanwhile, another Frenchman, Louis Blériot, had entered the picture. Blériot was a manufacturer of automobile headlights who had become passionately interested in flying. He had first tried building biplanes but he had little luck with them and turned instead to monoplanes.

After Latham's failure, Blériot decided to attempt the cross-Channel flight in his latest monoplane. But bad weather held him up until Latham was ready with his new plane.

Tensely the two fliers waited by the coast of France. Each kept one eye on the weather and the other on his rival. On Saturday night, July 24, Latham went to bed, leaving strict orders that he should be called if the wind dropped. The wind did drop but Latham's friends let him sleep peacefully on.

Blériot, however, was wakeful; a burn on his foot was troubling him. At 2:30, he noticed that the wind had slackened slightly, so he climbed into his automobile and drove out to the airfield. There, he had his plane brought out from under its tent and made ready. For the next half hour, he hobbled around on his crutch, watching the night sky.

At 3:30, just before dawn, he took off into the cool morning air and flew a couple of circles around the airfield to test his three-cylinder, twenty-five-horsepower engine. It had a tendency to overheat but it seemed to be running smoothly. Blériot landed before the overheating could begin. "Replace the fuel," he told his mechanic. "In ten minutes I start for England."

It was 4:35 when he took off and pointed his propeller out over the Channel. Latham's friends, watching from a distance, had assumed that

Blériot is kissed by his wife after his sensational monoplane flight from France to England.

Blériot was merely making practice hops. When they saw that he was heading out to sea, they rushed to wake Latham. Hurriedly he struggled into his flying clothes and had his Antoinette brought out. But by now the wind had risen again and was blowing too strongly for him to take off.

Blériot sat hunched over his controls with the air stream from the propeller whipping past his helmeted head. He had no compass, no instruments of any kind. But on he flew, holding to what he hoped was the right course.

"For ten minutes," he said later, describing the tense period after he left the French coast behind him, "I was alone, isolated, lost in the middle of the foamy sea, seeing nothing on the horizon, not even a boat. . . . These ten minutes seemed long to me, and, truly, I was happy to catch sight of . . . a gray line which detached itself from the sea. . . It was the English coast."

That gray line was the chalk face of Shakespeare Cliff, rising from the sea. A cross wind had pushed Blériot further to the east than he expected and he finally swooped down to a rough landing near Dover Castle, at almost the same spot where Blanchard and Jeffries had started their cross-Channel balloon flight in 1785. He had covered the twenty miles in thirty-seven minutes.

Two days later, Latham made his second attempt to cross the Channel. But his engine failed again and he crashed into the sea, less than a mile from the English coast.

Blériot became a hero. In London, 120,000 people flocked to see his plane. Latham was hailed as a gallant and courageous loser. The French were now the leaders in the new sport of flying and in August, 1909, they established their lead even more definitely.

In that month the first great air meet was held at Reims, France, and flying really came of age.

The meet lasted for a week and was packed with excitement. The Wrights were not there but six of their planes were, and practically every other important flying pioneer was present. Day after day, new records were set and then broken again. Henri Farman of France won the endurance prize by staying in the air more than three hours. Glenn Curtiss won a speed prize by averaging forty-three miles per hour, and Latham won the altitude prize, claiming he had flown at 1,200 feet. The judges said he had been no higher than five hundred.

The week was filled with a spirit of excitement and adventure, and the people at Reims often spoke about "aviator's luck" or the "charmed" lives of the fliers. For although at least four of the planes were damaged or wrecked, none of the pilots was killed. The pioneers in flight did seem to enjoy beginner's luck. Between 1891, when Lilienthal had flown his first glider, and the Reims meet in 1909, only four men had been killed in heavier-than-air accidents. But this record was not to last for long. In the single year of 1910, thirty-two men were killed.

As the fliers became more accomplished, public interest in flying grew steadily. Thousands of people had bought the *Daily Mail* to follow its account of the first cross-Channel flight. To increase its circulation even more, the *Mail* offered a prize of ten thousand pounds to the first person to fly from London to Manchester, a distance of two hundred miles, in twenty-four hours or less.

This prize produced the first long-distance, cross-country airplane race in history, and it was followed breathlessly by hundreds of thousands of people. The race started on April 3, 1910, when a young Englishman named Claude Grahame-White set out from London. His plane was a French Farman biplane powered by a fifty-horsepower rotary engine which drove a propeller set behind the wings. He flew for two hours and landed, half-frozen, at the town of Rugby, after a record-breaking flight of eighty-five miles.

After refueling and thawing himself out, Grahame-White took off again and got more than halfway to Manchester. But a combination of engine trouble and gusty winds forced him to give up his attempt to beat the twenty-four-hour deadline. Next day the wind flipped his Farman over and damaged it, and Grahame-White had to take it back to his base near London for repairs.

By Wednesday, April 27, Grahame-White was ready to try again. But now a competitor appeared. He was a Frenchman, Louis Paulhan, who had already set a world's altitude record of 4,165 feet at an international air meet which had been held that January in Los Angeles.

Paulhan was also flying a Farman, which he had had shipped to London. He spent all of Wednesday assembling it, helped by the designer, Henri Farman. At five in the afternoon, the plane was ready. Without even making a trial flight, Paulhan announced that he intended to take off and fly as far as he could before darkness set in. He had chartered a special train to guide him. Following the train, he got to Lichfield, more than halfway to Manchester, before darkness fell.

Grahame-White had decided that it was too windy to fly that day. But when he heard, at six o'clock, that Paulhan had started, he decided to set out in pursuit. He took off despite the heavy wind and flew about sixty miles before darkness forced him to land.

But he was still fifty-seven miles behind his rival. In a frantic effort to close the gap, he decided to risk something that was almost unheard of at the time: a night take-off. The airfield was only dimly lit by automobile headlights, but at 2:30 on Thursday morning Grahame-White made his take-off and vanished into the darkness.

By this time, much of England and many people in other countries were caught up in the excite-ment of the race. Some people who lived on the route to Manchester sat up all night, hoping to catch a glimpse of the fliers. French and British newspapers put out extra editions, announcing the latest news, and bulletins were posted in New York and Berlin.

Night flying, as Grahame-White discovered, was extremely hazardous. "A great difficulty presented itself," he said later, "in not knowing in the darkness whether I was ascending or not . . . but I soon became accustomed to watching closely the movements of my elevating plane, which was silhouetted before me against the sky . . . On I flew. The weirdness of the sensation can scarcely be described. I was alone in the darkness with the roar of my engine in my ears."

Grahame-White also had to land in the darkness and to do that he first had to locate a landing field. To help him, a friend had agreed to shine his automobile headlights on the wall of an inn which was situated on his line of flight. The flier managed to pick up this light, which told him where he was. Then he spotted a freight train and followed it into Rugby, where he landed.

By this time, the Englishman was only a dozen miles behind Paulhan, who had just left Lichfield. But a strong wind was blowing at Rugby and no one appeared to help Grahame-White when he landed. He had a fierce struggle with the wind on the ground and his plane was nearly wrecked. Meanwhile, Paulhan flew straight to Manchester, where a huge crowd greeted him.

By 1910, the Wright brothers, Curtiss, Farman and Blériot had, between them, more or less standardized the basic designs for airplanes. Anyone who wanted to build a plane could do it by imitating their designs. But many people had their own idea of what an airplane should be like, and they turned out a stream of weird and amazing contraptions which they hoped would make them famous. Most of these planes, of course, could not get off the ground, and they simply remained in the backyards where they were built.

But the fliers themselves kept making new jumps forward. In November, 1910, a young civilian pilot, Eugene Ely, flew a Curtiss plane off the deck of an American cruiser. Two months later, he performed the even more daring feat of landing on

A photomontage of Lincoln Beachey flying under the Niagara Falls bridge after spanning the cataract.

a platform built over the afterdeck of the U. S. S. *Pennsylvania*. These two stunts were the first steps on the way to the creation of an aircraft carrier.

Meanwhile the Wrights and Glenn Curtiss had both set up flying schools. They also formed exhibition teams which toured the United States, giving people in small towns their first glimpse of the airplane. The fliers were stunters and they performed the wildest tricks. At fairgrounds and racetracks and farm pastures, and other open spaces where a plane could take off, crowds watched in shuddering expectation to see what would happen to these daring young men.

The most spectacular of the stunters was a daredevil pilot named Lincoln Beachey. He joined the Curtiss exhibition team in 1910 and promptly wrecked two planes. But he went on to become, in Orville Wright's opinion, "the greatest aviator of all."

Beachey was a wild man in the air. One of his tricks was to scoop handkerchiefs off the airfield with his wing tip. He liked to seesaw along a row of hangars, sticking a wing into each one as he flew by. He also enjoyed flying under bridges.

But Beachey's luck could not last for ever. In 1913, a French stunt flier, Adolphe Pégoud, made the loop the loop famous. Beachey was angry because he had not thought of the stunt first and he became a fanatical looper, often performing the loop at suicidally low heights. At last, in 1915, the wings of his plane collapsed when he was flying at a San Francisco exhibition and, as more than fifty thousand people watched, he plunged to his death in the Bay.

Another American pilot, Calbraith P. Rodgers, became famous in 1911, when he set out to win a $50,000 prize for the first coast-to-coast flight across the United States. To win the prize, Rodgers had to fly from the Atlantic to the Pacific in less than thirty days. He made the attempt in a Wright biplane and, as he flew, a three-car train followed —and sometimes led—him across the country. It carrried his wife, his mother, mechanics and about four thousand dollars' worth of spare parts. Though Rodgers reached the Pacific, he was nineteen days too late to win the prize.

While airplanes and their pilots kept setting new records, travel in lighter-than-air machines was not forgotten. Between 1900 and 1910 ballooning made a comeback as a sport in the United States. Both the French and the British also made successful flights in airships. But the biggest ad-

Lincoln Beachey, the fabulous stunt flyer

vances were made in Germany by the most famous of all designers of dirigibles, Count Ferdinand von Zeppelin.

Zeppelin's first dirigible was launched in 1900 and reached a speed of sixteen miles per hour. His next dirigible, the *LZ-2,* was launched in 1905 and had much more powerful engines. It was wrecked by the wind after making only two voyages. But the German government was now becoming interested. After Zeppelin's next dirigible, the *LZ-3,* had made several successful flights, the German army agreed to buy an airship provided it could fly for twenty-four hours and make a round trip of at least 435 miles.

Zeppelin built a fourth dirigible to pass this test. It was forced down twice and, during the second stop for repairs, it was struck by a squall and dragged along the ground until it exploded in a sheet of flame. Zeppelin was in despair. But the catastrophe aroused the interest of the German people and they contributed nearly $1,500,000 to a Zeppelin fund. The government then decided to accept the *LZ-3,* and set about building several of them.

By 1910 people had become so confident about flying dirigibles that Zeppelin was able to start a dirigible passenger service. Five airships were used in the service. They had carpets and wicker armchairs, and lunches were served during the flight. Passengers by the thousands bought tickets to sail in comfort through the air at about forty-five miles per hour.

But it was a risky form of travel. Hydrogen was still as explosive as it had ever been and the dirigible's huge bulk made it especially vulnerable to storms and high winds. Of the twenty-six dirigibles that Zeppelin built before 1914, more than half were destroyed.

The most ambitious American designer of dirigibles was probably the journalist and explorer Walter Wellman. Like Zeppelin, Wellman had many unfortunate experiences with his airships. First he tried to build a small dirigible which would take him over the North Pole. He made two attempts, in 1907 and 1909, but they were both unsuccessful.

After Admiral Peary reached the Pole with dogsleds, Wellman decided to end his attempts to

Aides rush to extricate Calbraith Rodgers after one of 19 crashes on his coast-to-coast flight.

fly over the North Pole. Instead he decided to rebuild his airship, the *America,* and try to fly the Atlantic. He increased the airship's length, gave her two engines, and added a detachable lifeboat. He also designed a steel guide rope which weighed two tons and had drums of gasoline spaced at intervals along it. It was called an "equilibrator" and was intended to provide extra ballast.

With a crew of six and a small gray cat as mascot, Wellman set out from Atlantic City on October 15, 1910. Almost from the beginning, things went wrong. One engine failed eighty miles from the take-off. At night, the hydrogen contracted and the airship came down so low that it was almost rammed by a schooner.

The next morning, the wind rose and the waves tossed the equilibrator about so violently that it threatened to shake loose the gondola, which housed the crew, from the gas bag. At last, after an erratic flight of several hundred miles, the weary airmen sighted a steamer and Wellman decided to abandon ship.

Wellman was not the only man to dream of crossing the Atlantic Ocean by air. Airplane pilots were also thinking about it. In 1914, the *Daily Mail* offered a prize of $50,000 for the first successful non-stop trans-Atlantic flight. But in August, 1914, World War I broke out and civilian flying practically came to an end for four long years.

41

French pilot and observer demonstrate the wide arc of fire possessed by early pursuit planes.

World War I

AT the outbreak of war in August of 1914, the airplane was still a toy. Some planes could fly at more than 125 miles per hour. Others could climb as high as 25,000 feet, while still others could fly for more than a thousand miles without stopping. But high performance in one area usually ruled out capability in others.

Also, the airplane was still a very new invention and most government officials could not see what an important weapon it would be. "We do not consider," said the British Secretary for War, "that aeroplanes will be of any possible use for war purposes." These officials were reluctant to spend money on machines that had never been tried in battle. But there were some far-sighted officials in every country who did realize how useful the airplane would be in war, and they managed to get war planes built.

When the war began, the two sides were fairly evenly matched in the air. The Germans had about 1,200 combat planes, of which 260 were ready to fight. The British and French had about 1,000 combat planes, of which about 220 were ready for immediate combat.

In 1912, the British had organized a special Flying Corps. Like the Germans and the French, they assumed that planes would be most useful for directing artillery fire and carrying out reconnaissance over the enemy's front lines. Both sides therefore wanted slow, stable aircraft which would allow pilots to study and photograph the ground.

The main British reconnaissance plane was the BE-2. It was a steady, reliable biplane made by Captain Geoffrey de Havilland, a designer and test pilot who later started his own aircraft company. The BE-2 could carry two men, guns, and a camera at speeds up to seventy-five miles per hour, and it could stay aloft for three hours.

The British also had two single-seater planes, the Bristol Scout and the Sopwith Tabloid, which could fly at over ninety miles per hour. They used these faster planes to scout far back over the German lines and report on what preparations the Germans were making.

The French had similar planes. They used the fast Morane-Saulnier monoplane and the Nieuport biplane for scouting. They also had a slower Farman biplane for flying over the enemy's front positions and for directing their own artillery.

The Germans had several different heavy biplanes for artillery direction and front line reconnaissance. For scouting, they used the Albatros biplane and a monoplane which was named the Taube ("Dove") because its swept-back wings gave it a dove-like appearance.

Neither side particularly wanted fast planes at first. In fact, the German High Command actually held back the production of faster planes because higher speeds made taking photographs more difficult. Nor did the reconnaissance planes usually carry guns. They stuck to photography. If an Allied spotter met a German reconnaissance plane, the pilots were quite likely to wave cheerfully to each other as they went on with their jobs.

Almost from the start, both sides tried to use their planes for bombing. But their early efforts were very crude and did almost no damage. One German lieutenant dropped two four-pound bombs by hand while he was flying over the outskirts of

JOIN THE ARMY AIR SERVICE BE AN AMERICAN EAGLE !

CONSULT YOUR LOCAL DRAFT BOARD. READ THE ILLUSTRATED BOOKLET AT ANY RECRUITING OFFICE, OR WRITE TO THE CHIEF SIGNAL OFFICER OF THE ARMY, WASHINGTON, D.C.

A patriotic poster of World War I summons young Americans to join the new fighting arm.
Such posters and the drama of air battle caused Americans to volunteer by the thousands.

Paris. Another German pilot managed to drop a note behind the French lines stating that the German army was at the gates of Paris and that the people should surrender. He tied this note to an old cavalry boot so that it would fall straight and threw it out of his plane.

The Allies also began to use bombs soon after the war began. First, they sent some planes over Brussels, which had been occupied by the Germans. Then, on November 14, the British sent three planes to bomb Zeppelin sheds in south Germany.

The bombs did little damage to the Zeppelins and one of the British bombers was brought down. But the Germans retaliated quickly by forming a bombing squadron which they called the "Ostend Carrier Pigeons." By January, 1915, they were raiding Dunkirk, behind the Allied lines in France. These bombers flew in formation, and they flew at night, which was a big step forward in aerial technique.

Both sides were naturally eager to stop enemy bombers and reconnaissance planes from flying over their lines. The obvious way was to use the light scout planes as fighters to drive off the intruders. But to drive the enemy away, the scout planes needed guns and for several months their armament remained extremely primitive.

One British pilot had thought of turning his plane into a fighter less than three weeks after war broke out. He mounted a machine gun on his French Farman and tried to chase an enemy plane. But the Farman was unable to climb above 3,500 feet and the German plane got away. The pilot's commander decided that it was the weight of the machine gun which had kept the Farman down, and he ordered the pilot to leave guns to the infantry, where they belonged.

Another British pilot, Captain Lanoe Hawker, was more effective. Late in July, 1915, he took off in his Bristol Scout armed with a cavalry rifle. It was mounted on the starboard side of the fuselage and pointed outwards, away from the plane, so that the bullets would clear the propeller. Flying over Belgium, Hawker attacked three German two-seaters in succession. He had to control his plane with one hand and fire with the other. But he managed to shoot down two of the Germans.

This exploit was considered so daring that Hawker was awarded Britain's highest decoration for bravery, the Victoria Cross.

Hawker had to shoot sideways, from a platform that was moving at a target that was also moving. Few gunners were able to shoot so accurately under such conditions. What both sides needed was a gun that could fire straight forward so that the pilot could aim his whole plane at the enemy. This meant that the gun must somehow be able to shoot past the propeller.

As it happened, both the British and the French had experimented with machine guns which could fire past a moving propeller. An English inventor had patented such a device and sent it to the British War Office before the war. But there the idea was lost. The French had also tried out a similar device but the gun they used was not satisfactory, and they abandoned it.

It was a French pilot who came up with the first effective forward-firing gun. He was Roland Garros who, in 1913, had been the first man to fly across the Mediterranean. In February, 1915, Garros mounted a forward-firing automatic rifle close behind the propeller on his Morane monoplane. There was a very good chance that many of the bullets would hit the propeller, and so it was armored with triangular steel plates in order to deflect bullets.

The German pilots did not know that Garros had a forward-firing gun, and they did not bother to take evasive action when they saw him flying toward them head on. Within sixteen days, he shot down five German planes.

Garros' advantage lasted until April 19, 1915. Then engine trouble forced him to land behind the enemy lines. The Germans captured both him and his plane (though he later escaped) and the armored propeller was closely examined.

Since early in the war, the Germans had been employing a brilliant Dutch airplane designer named Anthony Fokker. After examining Garros' plane, the Germans showed it to Fokker and told him either to duplicate it or to come up with something better.

Fokker had never seen a machine gun in his life. But he returned to his factory with the gun captured from Garros and a standard German machine gun. Garros had fired through his propeller blades at random and thus taken the chance of hitting his own propeller. Fokker came up with a better idea. In two days, he designed a rod-and-lever mechanism which synchronized the firing of the gun with the revolving of the blades, so that the bullets would miss the propeller.

Fokker installed the device on one of his monoplanes and demonstrated it successfully to a group of German officers. But the officers insisted that Fokker must personally test his weapon in action. A few days later, the Dutchman took off under protest, and soon got a French Farman in his gun sights. Then, abruptly, he decided not to shoot. As he explained later: "I had no wish to kill Frenchmen for Germans. Let them do their own killing."

Fokker's device was not a complete success. The brilliant German pilot Max Immelmann shot his own propeller off twice while using it. But it did give the Germans superiority in the air for several months. In fact, the device was so effective that the Allies began to call it "Fokker's scourge."

Searching for a counter-weapon, the British stepped up production of a plane with the propeller situated in the rear so that the gunner could fire forward freely. For a while the French

continued to use Garros' forward-firing gun, but several of their pilots shot themselves down. Then the French tried mounting a machine gun on the top wing of their Nieuports and firing over the propeller. This gave the pilots a clear field of fire but the position of the gun increased air resistance and slowed down the plane.

The risk of being shot down became so great that no Allied reconnaissance planes dared to venture over the German lines without a heavy escort. Meanwhile, the Germans were terribly afraid that their secret and deadly weapon might fall into Allied hands. They therefore forbade any plane carrying the Fokker device to fly over enemy territory. But in April, 1916, a German pilot got lost in the fog and landed by mistake behind the Allied lines. The plane was captured, Fokker's design was carefully examined, and his device was immediately copied by the British and French.

As the war progressed, each side produced a number of remarkable fighter pilots who became known as "aces." This was a word used by the French to describe a person who was outstanding in any field. But as the war went on, it came to be

A French Maurice Farman biplane cruises over the battlefront near the beginning of World War I.

Famous Airplanes: 1914-1918

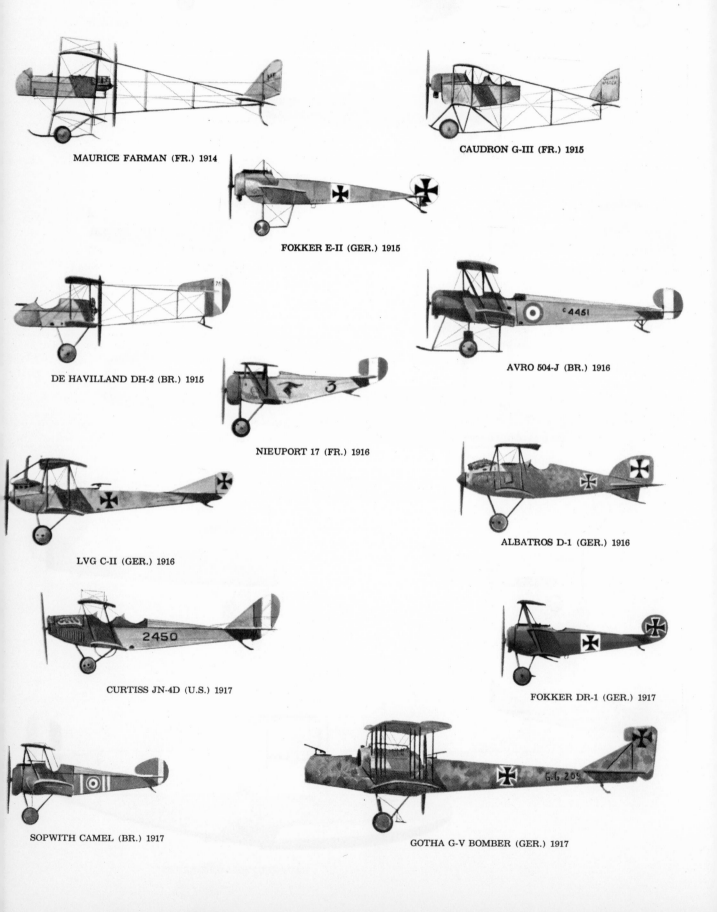

MAURICE FARMAN (FR.) 1914

CAUDRON G-III (FR.) 1915

FOKKER E-II (GER.) 1915

DE HAVILLAND DH-2 (BR.) 1915

AVRO 504-J (BR.) 1916

NIEUPORT 17 (FR.) 1916

LVG C-II (GER.) 1916

ALBATROS D-1 (GER.) 1916

CURTISS JN-4D (U.S.) 1917

FOKKER DR-1 (GER.) 1917

SOPWITH CAMEL (BR.) 1917

GOTHA G-V BOMBER (GER.) 1917

BRISTOL F-2B (BR.) 1917

SPAD 13 (FR.) 1917

BREGUET 14 (FR.) 1917

SE-5 (BR.) 1917

FOKKER D-VII (GER.) 1918

HANDLEY PAGE 0/400 (BR.) 1917

JUNKERS D-1 (GER.) 1918

AMERICAN DH-4 (BR.-U.S.) 1918

LOENING M-8 (U.S.) 1918

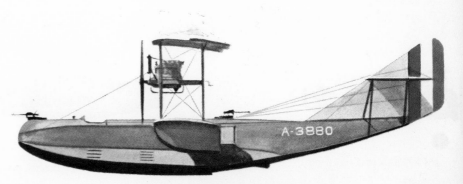

NAVY-CURTISS F-5L (U.S.) 1918

used mainly to apply to fighter pilots. The French gave the title "ace" to any pilot who shot down five enemy planes. The Germans granted the title only to a pilot who shot down ten planes. Both the Allies and the Germans insisted that each "kill" should be seen by at least three witnesses. So most of the aces probably shot down many more planes than were officially claimed for them.

The aces were a mixed group. One of the most famous, the Englishman Albert Ball, was a dreamy-eyed youth who raised rabbits and vegetables around the airfield to keep his mind off the war. In his letters, he assured his parents that he always remembered to say his prayers. Yet he was a deadly killer in the air and shot down forty-four enemy planes before he disappeared.

No one is quite sure how Ball died but one story is that he developed a habit of flying low over a certain church-tower in German-occupied territory to see what time it was. The Germans noticed this habit and hid a machine gun in the tower which shot down the unsuspecting Englishman.

British top fighter ace, Edward Mannock

There were aces from almost every country which fought in the war. The first ace, Roland Garros, was a Frenchman. Another French ace, Georges Guynemer, was shot down seven times before he disappeared in 1917. The Canadian, Billy Bishop, was awarded the Victoria Cross for attacking a German airfield single-handed. The Belgian ace Willy Coppens once landed on a German observation balloon and took off again. And a Russian ace, A. A. Kazakov, who shot down seventeen planes, destroyed his first German Albatros by ramming it with his own undercarriage.

The Americans produced their aces, too. One was Lieutenant Eddie Rickenbacker, a former automobile racing driver, who shot down 26 planes between April and November, 1918. Rickenbacker was famous for his icy nerves. "He couldn't," said a fellow American ace, "put as many holes in a target that was being towed as I could, but he could put more holes in a target that was shooting at him than I could."

The most colorful American combat flier was probably Frank Luke, who was known as the "balloon buster from Arizona." Some of Luke's senior officers disliked him because he often ignored orders. But no one ever questioned his courage. Five times he brought his plane back so full of bullet holes that it had to be retired from combat. By late September, 1918, he had become the leading American ace. But he ignored orders once too often, and on September 29 his commanding officer told Luke that he would not be allowed to fly again until he learned to obey orders.

Eddie Rickenbacker, America's leading air ace, shot down 26 enemy planes within a few months.

Luke was so angry that he took off in his French Spad without permission and headed for enemy territory. An order was issued for his arrest but the arrest was never made. Luke refueled at a forward airfield and, late that afternoon, he flew over an American balloon headquarters and dropped a note. It said, "Watch three Hun balloons on the Meuse. Luke."

After delivering this message, Luke went after the balloons himself. He destroyed the first and was badly wounded while shooting down the second. Still he kept on and shot down the third. He then shot up some German soldiers on the ground before he was forced to land—probably through faintness from loss of blood.

German troops surrounded him and called on him to surrender. But Luke refused to surrender and fought on with his revolver until he was killed by rifle fire. He had carried out his last mission in defiance of orders but his courage was so great that he was posthumously awarded the highest American award for gallantry, the Medal of Honor.

One British ace, Edward Mannock, shot down 73 planes. The French ace René Fonck shot down 75. Both these men were remarkable pilots. But the two greatest fliers of the war were probably both Germans.

The better known of the two, Manfred Von Richthofen, became famous as the leader of the "flying circus," the most deadly group of fighter pilots in the war. Richthofen shot down 80 planes before his death in April, 1918. Perhaps his most famous victory was the one over the English flier Lanoe Hawker. While British and German soldiers below watched in breathless excitement, the two men fought from 10,000 down to 150 feet above the ground. Finally a bullet from Richthofen's red Albatros creased Hawker's skull and the unconscious pilot crashed to his death.

The other great German ace, Oswald Boelcke, had once been a schoolmaster. He was a keen student of the theory of aerial combat as well as a deadly fighter. He picked his pilots carefully and took a great deal of trouble to teach them combat

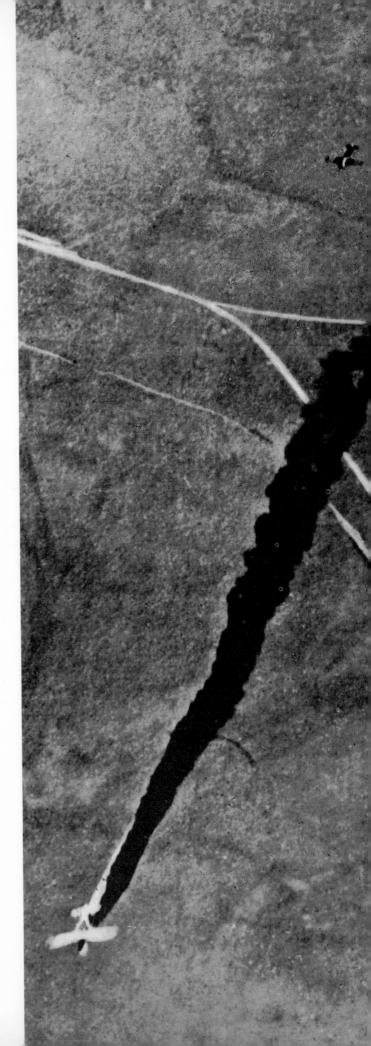

Painting by a French artist shows a quieter side of aerial warfare: training and maintenance.

tactics, such as how to use clouds for cover, how to make use of the wind, and how to take an enemy by surprise by suddenly swooping down on him from out of the sun.

No one seemed able to defeat Boelcke, and his squadron mates came to believe that he was invincible in the air. But in October, 1916, when he was leading an attack against two British planes, Boelcke suffered a fatal stroke of bad luck. One of his pupils brushed the wing of his plane against his leader's Albatros; the plane fell out of control, and Boelcke was killed.

Even his enemies were saddened. Pilots of the British Flying Corps flew over his grave and

A French hydroplane, bombing from less than 200 feet above the sea, destroys a German submarine.

dropped a wreath inscribed to "our brave and chivalrous foe." This inscription was sincere, for the fighter pilots of each side fought with a sense of chivalry and kinship. Although they were enemies, they shared the same risks. A wing could come off in a dive; a single bullet could turn a gasoline tank into a blazing inferno. Sharing these risks formed a tie which bound all fighter pilots, of whatever country, together.

By 1916 both the German and the Allied High Commands had come to understand the importance of the airplane in battle. They realized that if one side could only win superiority in the air, the commanders on the other side would be "blinded," for they would not be able to find out what the enemy was doing behind his lines. But until the last few months of the war, neither side was able to win this superiority and the generals argued furiously over how best to use their planes.

Both sides also made important use of seaplanes and flying boats for reconnaissance over the ocean, and for bombing and torpedo attacks against ships. It was a British seaplane which, in May of 1915, warned Admiral Beatty of the approach of the German fleet at Jutland, where the greatest naval battle of the war was to be fought. And by the end of the war, the British had seaplanes which could cross the North Sea and shoot down Zeppelins patrolling the German coast.

Bombers, too, gradually became more effective. When the war began, the closest thing either side had to a bomber were the two-seater reconnaissance planes from which the navigator dropped hand grenades or, sometimes, bricks. Then the British developed light bombers which could carry 450 pounds of bombs underneath the wings, and a heavy, twin-engined bomber, the Handley Page 0/400 which could carry 1,800 pounds of bombs. The Germans had a similar plane, the Gotha. By the end of the war the British had produced a number of four-engined planes which could each carry 7,500 pounds of bombs. They could fly as far as Berlin, the German capital, and were ready to do so when the war ended.

All these advances were spurred on by the needs of war. While they were taking place, the United States, which had remained at peace, lagged further and further behind. The United States had been slow to realize how important warplanes would be. In 1908 the government had bought its first plane from the Wright brothers and for three years that one plane made up the entire United States air force. In 1911, money was provided to buy five more planes. By the end of 1913, the U. S. Army had still bought only twenty-eight planes and nine of them had crashed.

By this time about forty officers of the Signal Corps had been trained as pilots and eleven of them had been killed. The survivors thought their commanders were incompetent and they wrote a letter of complaint to Washington. The senior officers of the Signal Corps were furious and the Chief Signal Officer described the fliers as "deficient in discipline and the proper knowledge of the customs of the service and the duties of an officer."

The real trouble was that the senior officers of the Army did not understand the importance of airplanes. And the airplanes themselves were inefficient. This was proved in March, 1916, after the Mexican leader, Pancho Villa, crossed the Rio Grande and killed eighteen Americans. The American commander, General Pershing, set off to pursue the Mexicans and eight planes were given to him to help in the chase. It turned out to be the planes that needed help. They were battered by dust storms, windstorms, and snowstorms and proved unable to fly over the Mexican mountains. In the end, all they were used for was to carry messages.

By April, 1916, the Army had only two airplanes left and neither was fit for service. The situation was so bad that Congress ordered thirteen million dollars spent on military aviation. But providing the money turned out to be easier than getting the planes. For the manufacturers simply did not have the equipment necessary to build so many aircraft. Although 366 planes were ordered in 1916, only 64 were delivered.

The United States entered the European war on April 6, 1917. It did not have a separate air force, only an Aviation Section of the Signal Corps. This section contained 131 officers, most of them pilots, and about 1,000 enlisted men. It possessed fewer than 250 airplanes. Even worse, the United States was not able to build up its air

A Caudron biplane drops smoke fuses to illuminate German positions at the Battle of Verdun.

force rapidly. The Curtiss airplane company was the only one which possessed a real factory; all the other plants were extremely small. And although there were about a dozen good aeronautical engineers in the country, none of them knew how to design an up-to-date fighting plane.

At first the government did not realize just how bad the situation was. Within a few days after the U. S. entered the war, Allied officials began to arrive, clamoring for planes. Dazzling plans were drawn up to meet their requests. One program called for 22,625 planes to be built. Another plan was that 263 American squadrons should be in action by June, 1918.

Second-ranking French ace, Georges Guynemer, sends two German fliers hurtling from their planes.

But soon these plans were scaled down and some sensible decisions were made. One was that the U. S. should mass-produce just a few battle-tested kinds of aircraft, such as the three-engined Italian Caproni bomber, the Handley Page 0/400 heavy bomber, and the DH-4 light bomber. A few American Curtiss flying boats were also ordered, and an American training plane, the Curtiss JN-4D (the Jenny), was mass-produced. Actually, the most important American technical contribution to the war in the air was the twelve-cylinder Liberty engine which developed 400 horsepower and was used to power the DH-4's and the Handley Page 0/400's.

Meanwhile, thousands of Americans had to be trained to fly, and nearly all the Allied instructors who had experience in battle were in Europe. The American student pilots were therefore shipped over to Europe and about 2,500 were trained there by the end of the war.

They were not the first Americans to fly in battle. From 1916 on, a number of American volunteers had been flying with the French air force.

A highly-maneuverable German W-29 seaplane machine guns a stricken English Curtiss flying boat.

Their group was known as the Lafayette Escadrille and they had two lion cubs called ''Whiskey'' and ''Soda'' as mascots. About 180 Americans flew in this group and nearly a third of them were killed, but they shot down 199 German planes.

By April, 1918, the new American squadrons were beginning to go into action. The first daylight bombing squadron began its operations in June, 1918. And in July, American fliers were organized into a special brigade and given the job of looking after their own section of the front line.

The commander of the American air force was a former officer of the Signal Corps named Billy Mitchell. He took up flying in 1915 when he was thirty-six years old, and, when the U. S. declared war on Germany, he was in Europe as an observer. He was the first pilot wearing an American uniform to fly over the enemy lines. His job was to send reports back to Washington, describing how the Allies were fighting the war, and his reports were so thorough and perceptive that he became the obvious choice to command America's aerial combat forces.

Mitchell was an extremely far-sighted officer. He agreed with the British air force commander, General Trenchard, that the airplane could win wars if it was used as an offensive weapon to bomb and cripple enemy war factories. Both men agreed that the air force should not be left under the command of army officers. Instead airplanes should be concentrated in massive formations under the command of independent air force generals.

But Mitchell went even further than Trenchard. He dreamed of a great offensive to be carried out by men from the air. His plan was to lift thousands of men into the air, ten to each plane, and drop them by parachute behind the unsuspecting enemy.

This plan was never carried out during World War I. Both Trenchard and Mitchell were looking ahead to the future. For, despite the glamour of flying, air power did not really play a very important part in World War I. Airplanes were useful for reconnaissance, yet even this use was limited. Important targets such as army headquarters were often covered or disguised so that they could not be identified from the air. This use of cover was called camouflage and it kept observer planes from seeing what lay beneath.

Planes were sometimes used to machine-gun or bomb enemy troops, and a determined pilot could do a lot of damage. For example, Ernst Udet is supposed to have knocked out a British tank, diving on it six times until it was destroyed. This kind of low-level attack was dangerous for the planes and pilots; the planes were comparatively slow and therefore easy to shoot down.

Until very late in the war, the bombing of enemy industries was not very effective either. There were not enough planes to do the job properly and their bombing was not accurate enough. Not a single important industry was put out of action by bombing. But right from the outbreak of war, the Allies were worried about the bombing that might be done by German Zeppelins.

Most of the German Zeppelins which raided England were commanded by a man of great courage named Peter Strasser. At first Strasser used his airships mainly to keep a lookout for British ships in the North Sea. But in August, 1915, the Germans began to launch Zeppelin bombing attacks on London. These attacks were always made at night and always in the dark of the moon. One Zeppelin commander, Heinrich Mathy, made thirteen raids on England and in one raid he set off fires which did $2,500,000 worth of damage.

This was the most destructive bombing raid of the war. By the fall of 1916 British planes had learned how to shoot down the airships, and in one raid they shot down four out of eleven attackers. When an airship was hit, it often burst into flames. The sight of a fellow dirigible being ripped by fire was terrifying to the crews of the other Zeppelins and they sometimes became so unnerved that they dropped their bombs at random and raced for home.

On August 5, 1918, Strasser himself led five Zeppelins against England. He flew in the new LZ-70, a giant airship which could fly as fast as eighty-two miles per hour. But the British had heavily armed fighter planes waiting. Before the LZ-70 could even reach the British coast, she went down under the guns of a DH-4. Strasser was killed and, with his death, the Zeppelin organization fell apart.

The only known photograph of a Zeppelin armada in action shows them on a bombing raid over England.

By this time, however, the war was nearing its end. In September and October, 1918, the Allies launched a series of great attacks against the German lines. They outnumbered the Germans in the air as well as on the ground and their attacks were supported by well over a thousand airplanes, including hundreds of American planes.

Some of the planes attacked the German troops in their front line trenches. Others struck at German fighters and swept them out of the sky. Meanwhile the heavy bombers dropped their bombs on German trains and supply lines far behind the front.

These bombing attacks were very different from the flying operations in the early days of the war. Then, pilots on reconnaissance missions had waved to enemy fliers in the friendly comradeship of the sky. Since then, flying had become less individual and the aerial fighting had grown organized and ruthless. The bombing attacks at the end of the war were carried out by dozens of bombers which flew in tight formation and drenched the target area with their bombs.

No one knows how much damage these raids did. Undoubtedly they reduced the German soldiers' will to fight. But they were even more important for the glimpse they gave into the future. To anyone with foresight, the lesson was clear: *If you hold the air, you cannot be beaten; if you lose the air, you cannot win.*

Famous Airplanes: 1919-1927

CURTISS NC-4 1919

JUNKERS F-13 (GER.) 1919

CURTISS ORIOLE 1920

DAYTON-WRIGHT RACER 1920

MARTIN MB-2 1921

BURNELLI RB-2 1924

TRAVEL AIR 1924

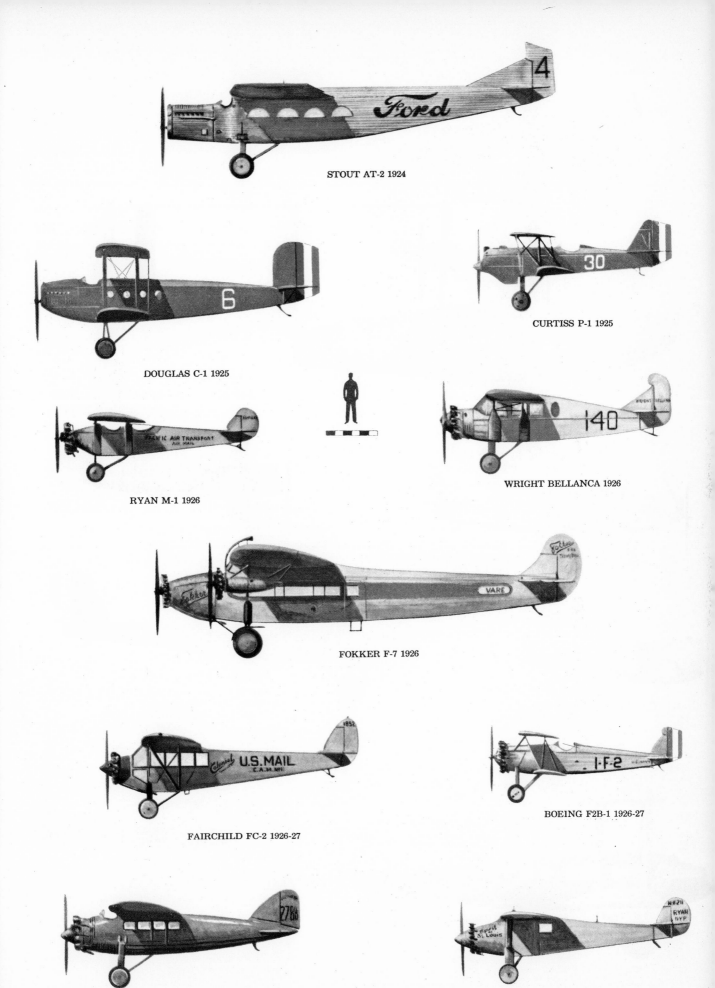

STOUT AT-2 1924

CURTISS P-1 1925

DOUGLAS C-1 1925

RYAN M-1 1926

WRIGHT BELLANCA 1926

FOKKER F-7 1926

FAIRCHILD FC-2 1926-27

BOEING F2B-1 1926-27

LOCKHEED VEGA 1927

RYAN SPIRIT OF ST. LOUIS 1927

One of many fighting scenes out on a wing which helped add drama to Hollywood movies of the 1920's.

The Twenties

A S long as the war lasted, aviation prospered in the United States. Thousands of young men learned to fly, airfields were built by the score, and factories were swamped with orders for airplanes. But when the war came to an end, the situation abruptly changed.

For one thing, the government no longer needed its military planes and was ready to sell them at almost any price. With so many planes going cheap, manufacturers could not sell new ones, and so they stopped building them. The pilots, too, were in trouble. For when the war ended, most of the fliers were dismissed from the Army and found themselves without jobs.

Yet in many ways, the years just after the war were the most exciting in the whole history of flight. In order to make a living, many pilots became acrobats of the air, and they made flying more glamorous than it had ever been before.

These aerial acrobats were called barnstormers. They used war-surplus DH-4's and Curtiss Jenny training planes for their stunts. In these planes, they hopped from one town to the next, performing at carnivals, country fairs, and wherever else crowds gathered to be entertained in the open air.

As the years passed, many barnstormers shifted to safer jobs. Some went back into the Army or Navy. Others set up flying schools. Still others began to use their planes to carry freight or passengers, and thereby paved the way for the commercial airlines of today.

The Europeans were the first to set up services for carrying passengers by air. By the beginning of 1919, a German airline was running flights between three major cities. In Holland, the designer Anthony Fokker quickly built factories to produce commercial planes, and the Dutch airline KLM was started in 1919. In the same year, the British and French both organized passenger flights between London and Paris.

Organizing passenger flights was more difficult in the United States. The big cities were further apart and many were separated by mountains. The first U. S. commercial airline, which was formed in 1919, carried passengers only between New York and Atlantic City. Soon afterwards, the company moved its headquarters to Miami and began to fly passengers to the Bahamas, while a rival company set up flights between Miami and Havana.

The early passenger planes could carry only a few people and the fares they charged did not cover the cost of the flights. Several European countries were eager to develop commercial airlines, so they gave the companies money to help them stay in business. But the United States government was unwilling to subsidize the companies. It was afraid of exerting too much control and interfering with private enterprise.

But eventually it became clear that the passenger services could not survive without government help. Finally, the government came up with a solution. It would use the private companies to help deliver the mail and pay them heavily for doing so.

Actually the Post Office had first tried to fly the mail in its own planes. From the start, it had run into trouble. In May, 1918, a pilot who was supposed to fly mail from Washington to Philadelphia got lost on the way. He flew to southeastern Maryland instead, and the mail eventually had to be sent on to Philadelphia by train.

By the summer of 1919, Post Office pilots were flying from New York to Chicago over the storm-swept Allegheny mountains. The route was known as the "graveyard run" because it was so dangerous. The pilots flew in open cockpits with no radio beams to guide them, no instruments to help them find direction in the dark, without even lighted beacons on the ground to show them the way. Usually they navigated by following railway tracks and hoping that the track would not suddenly disappear into a tunnel.

But the worst danger was the cold. "The planes were drafty," one airmail pilot explained, "and the first ones had poor windshields and holes in the bottom around the base of the stick, and the temperatures would get below zero. Pretty soon, you'd sit there and you couldn't move much. I'm sure this resulted in some accidents because pilots got so bitterly cold and numb that their judgment was poor."

The combination of dark and cold and lack of instruments made some mail trips as dangerous as flying in combat. Of the first forty pilots hired by the Post Office, thirty-one were killed.

It was not until 1925 that the Congress finally passed a law allowing the government to use private airlines to carry the mail. This law gave American flying a tremendous boost. The mail runs were enormously profitable and the private lines bid eagerly for contracts. To carry out their contracts, the companies needed more planes and, for the first time since the end of the war, aircraft manufacturers began to receive big orders.

As air traffic grew heavier, the government realized that some way of regulating flights was needed. So in May of 1926 Congress passed the Air Commerce Act which became the basis of commercial aviation in the United States. The act created a Bureau of Aeronautics to license all American planes and pilots, set up rules for air traffic, and test new engines and aircraft for safety.

Meanwhile a tremendous struggle had been going on over military aircraft. The central figure in this fight was General Billy Mitchell, who had commanded the American air forces during the war. When the war ended, Mitchell did everything he could to keep up interest in flying. For example,

he arranged an aerial watch against forest fires on the West Coast and a flying border patrol along the Rio Grande. But the government wanted to spend as little money as possible and none was available for new and better planes. So the Army pilots had to keep flying the old wartime DH-4's. Between the middle of 1920 and the middle of 1921, 330 Army planes crashed and 69 fliers were killed.

Mitchell was furious. Through newspapers and magazines, he waged a tremendous campaign for better aircraft. One of his arguments was that airplanes had become more important than warships, because ships could be sunk from the air. He kept insisting that his bombers could sink any warship afloat, and he kept offering to prove it.

In June and July, 1921, Mitchell finally got his chance. About seventy miles off the mouth of Chesapeake Bay, a group of former German warships was anchored, and it was agreed that they should be used to test the airplane's power against ships. The first attack was made by Navy seaplanes against a German submarine which quickly went down. Then Army planes quickly sank a destroyer and a light cruiser. But the really important target was a battleship, the *Ostfriesland,* which many people considered unsinkable. It had survived severe damage from mines and guns during the Battle of Jutland, and was one of the most heavily armored ships in the world.

The first attacks on the *Ostfriesland* were carried out with light bombs and they hardly damaged the giant battleship. Then planes attacked with 1,000-pound bombs which also had little

Passengers descending from an Armstrong-Whitworth Argosy after their flight from London to Paris.

The United States Navy's NC-4 was the first plane to span the Atlantic. Painting shows it swooping low over Plymouth Hoe, England, after flying from Newfoundland via the Azores and Portugal.

effect. But Mitchell had prodded the Army into developing bombs which weighed 2,000 pounds. Flying at 2,500 feet, a formation of eight Martin bombers each dropped one of these giant bombs. They fell in the water around the *Ostfriesland,* and the impact of their underwater explosions shattered the ship's hull. Within twenty-five minutes the battleship sank beneath the waves.

Some senior Naval officers were quick to learn the lesson. "We must put planes on battleships," announced Rear Admiral Moffett, the new Chief of Naval Aviation, "and get aircraft carriers quickly." Eight months later, the first carrier, the U.S.S. *Langley,* was commissioned for service with the fleet.

But Mitchell was not satisfied. He believed that aircraft carriers could be sunk as easily as battleships and he did not think that the nation's air power should be left under the control of admirals and generals. He kept up his campaign for an independent air force and he found many people to agree with him, for the airplane had made advances even in the few years since the end of the war. Every year they were able to fly longer distances. There were, for example, the Navy flying boats designed by Glenn Curtiss. Soon after the war ended, the Navy decided to show off these planes by sending three of them across the Atlantic to England.

The route chosen lay across Newfoundland, the Azores, and Portugal. On May 6, 1919, the NC-1 (Navy Curtiss number 1), NC-3, and NC-4 left Newfoundland on the first leg of the journey. The NC-1 had bad luck. It became lost in the fog and landed some two hundred miles west of the Azores, where the crew was picked up and the plane was abandoned.

The NC-3 also had bad luck. Two hundred and five miles from the Azores, she landed on seas so rough that she could not take off again. But, by a wonderful feat of navigation, her commander managed to half-sail, half-taxi the plane to the Azores and safety. The NC-4 was faster and luckier than her sister planes. Although fog blanketed the sea near the Azores, she landed safely, after covering the 1,380 miles at an average speed of 74.8 knots. From there, she went on triumphantly to Portugal and England.

But this feat, with its stop midway across the Atlantic, still left the old *Daily Mail* prize, offered in 1913, to be won. It called for a non-stop flight between the British Isles and the New World. The task was formidable. More than 1,800 miles of stormy ocean lay between Ireland and Newfoundland. Even with a tail wind to help, a loaded plane could not average much more than one hundred miles an hour. During the flight, it would probably be cut off from all communication with the ground. Radio communications were still so unreliable that pilots often preferred to fly without radio equipment on long flights in order to save weight.

A month after the flight of the NC-4, two Britons decided to try for the prize. They were Captain John Alcock and Lieutenant Arthur Brown. Flying a remodelled two-engine bomber, they took off from St. John's, Newfoundland, on June 14. The weather was appalling but they kept flying for nearly sixteen and a half hours, and when they finally crash-landed in an Irish bog they had won the *Daily Mail* prize.

Also in 1919, another daring pilot hazarded his life to win a prize. This prize was worth ten thousand pounds. It was offered by the Australian government to any Australian pilot who could fly from London to Australia in thirty days in a British-built airplane.

The Australian war flier Captain Ross Smith left England on November 12, in the same type of bomber which Alcock and Brown had used. Between Calcutta, India, and Australia there practically no usable airfields. The weather was bad all the way. But Smith and his crew landed at Darwin in northern Australia with fifty-two hours to spare and so were able to claim the prize.

All these feats had aroused tremendous public interest. So, when he started his campaign for an independent air force, General Billy Mitchell decided to win the public's support by showing them what his pilots could do.

His pilots smashed records right and left. In September, 1922, Lieutenant James Doolittle became the first person to fly across the United States in less than a day. With only one stop, he flew from Florida to California in twenty-one hours and twenty minutes.

In the following year, two other army pilots, Lieutenants John Macready and Oakley Kelly, made the first cross-country non-stop flight in just under twenty-seven hours. And in June, 1924, Lieutenant Russell Maughan flew from Long Island to San Francisco in just under eighteen hours, including stops to refuel. Because the sun rises in New York before it does in California, Maughan was able to begin and end his flight in daylight. He landed just at sunset and proudly handed the Mayor of San Francisco a copy of the *New York Times* that had been printed the same day.

Meanwhile three other Army planes were making a mass flight around the world. Early in April, 1924, eight of the Air Service's best pilots had set out from Seattle in four single-engine biplanes that could fly as either landplanes or seaplanes. Before the end of the month, one of them, the *Seattle,* crashed into a mountainside in Alaska. The other three planes continued on across the Pacific Ocean, Asia, and Europe. But while crossing the Atlantic, the *Boston* developed a faulty oil pump and had to be abandoned at sea. The remaining two planes flew on to Seattle and landed there on September 28, after flying 26,345 miles in under six months.

General Billy Mitchell, the man who proved battleships were vulnerable to attack from the air.

These feats were still not enough to satisfy Mitchell. He remained deeply worried about the weakness of American air power. Touring the Far East, he was disturbed by the inadequacy of American defenses at Pearl Harbor, the great naval base in the Pacific. "If your warships there," he wrote, "were to be found bottled up in a surprise attack from the air and our airplanes destroyed on the ground, nothing but a miracle would enable us to hold our Far East possessions."

Mitchell's prophecy was to be borne out some sixteen years later when the Japanese attacked Pearl Harbor and sank much of the American fleet. But at the time, government leaders were enraged by Mitchell's criticism. When his period of office as Assistant Chief of the Air Staff ended, he was not reappointed. Instead he was sent to command an obscure air base in Texas.

The Navy had also been irritated by Mitchell's criticisms and its leaders decided to show that its air power, at least, was in good condition. First the Navy sent a seaplane on a hazardous non-stop flight from San Francisco to Hawaii. But the plane ran out of fuel before it reached Hawaii and was forced to land in the ocean. Luckily the crew was picked up by a submarine.

The Navy also arranged for its dirigible, the *Shenandoah,* to make a series of appearances in the Midwest. While doing so, the airship was caught in a squall on September 3, 1925. First it was driven up to over 3,000 feet, then dropped down to 150 feet, then pushed up again. The *Shenandoah* could not stand this battering; it came apart in the air and fourteen members of its crew were killed.

Mitchell was disgusted by these disasters and accused both the Navy and the War Departments of "incompetency, criminal negligence, and almost treasonable administration" of aviation affairs. For this attack, he was court-martialled on a charge of insubordination. He was found guilty and when his conviction was confirmed he resigned from the Army.

While these arguments raged, the designers continued to make improvements in their planes. Perhaps the most enterprising was the German Hugo Junkers. During the war, he had developed a cantilevered wing which did not need any struts or braces to support it. A single wing was preferable to a double wing because it created less wind resistance and Junkers' invention revolutionized aircraft design. Once wings could be built without struts, the monoplane gradually began to replace the biplane.

Junkers was also the first man to build all-metal planes. Like other designers, he used corrugated metal. But another German designer, Adolph Rohrbach, realized that corrugated metal created resistance and in 1919 he began making planes with smooth-metal surfaces. Later designers went a step further. They learned that if they made the smooth surface of the wings strong enough, they could increase the weight which the wings would support.

It was the daring flights and the exciting races which did most to arouse the public's interest in aviation. The best known of the aerial races was probably the annual competition for the Schneider trophy. It had been started by Jacques Schneider of France in 1913 and was open to seaplanes of all nations.

The first purely racing planes did not appear until 1923, when the United States won the trophy with a Curtiss CR-3, the first plane to fly with a metal propeller. Its speed was 177 miles per hour. In 1925, James Doolittle won with a Curtiss biplane which he flew at 235 miles per hour. This was the last biplane to win the trophy. Later in the 1920's, the British came up with a series of streamlined monoplanes known as Supermarines. Flying them at well over 300 miles per hour, British pilots won the trophy three times running. Their three consecutive wins allowed the British to retire the Schneider trophy in 1931.

The pilots of bigger planes also had their triumphs. In 1926, Commander Richard Byrd and his pilot, Floyd Bennett, made the first flight over the North Pole, in a three-engined Fokker. The trip was especially dangerous because there were no landmarks in the frozen wastes to guide the fliers. During the flight, one of the engines began to leak oil but the plane stayed aloft and returned triumphantly, after a sixteen-hour flight. A few days later, the Norwegian explorer Roald Amundsen flew over the North Pole in a dirigible, the *Norge.*

Jimmy Doolittle stands on a pontoon of the R3C-2 in which he had won the 1925 Schneider Trophy.

But all these feats were to be dwarfed by the greatest and most famous flight in history. Its story began in 1919 when Raymond Orteig, the owner of a hotel in New York, offered a prize of $25,000 "to the first aviator who shall cross the Atlantic in a land or water aircraft (heavier-than-air) from Paris or the shores of France to New York, or from New York to Paris or the shores of France, without stop." The prize went unclaimed for seven years. There were plenty of men with enough courage to try crossing the Atlantic nonstop, and plenty of planes with strong enough wings. The trouble was that no one came up with an engine which could be relied on to run continuously for such a long distance.

On his trip to the North Pole, Commander Byrd had used three air-cooled 220-horsepower Wright Whirlwind engines. They were light, reliable, and efficient over long distances, and they caught the attention of a tall young airmail pilot named Charles Lindbergh, who worked in St. Louis. It occurred to Lindbergh that the Whirlwind engine might be powerful enough to pull a carefully designed monoplane across the 3,300-mile stretch from New York to Paris.

Although he was only twenty-four, Lindbergh was an extremely experienced pilot, with more than 2,000 hours in the air. He was an ex-barnstormer and wing-walker, and he had survived several parachute jumps. Unluckily, he had only

Famous Airplanes: U.S.–1928-1939

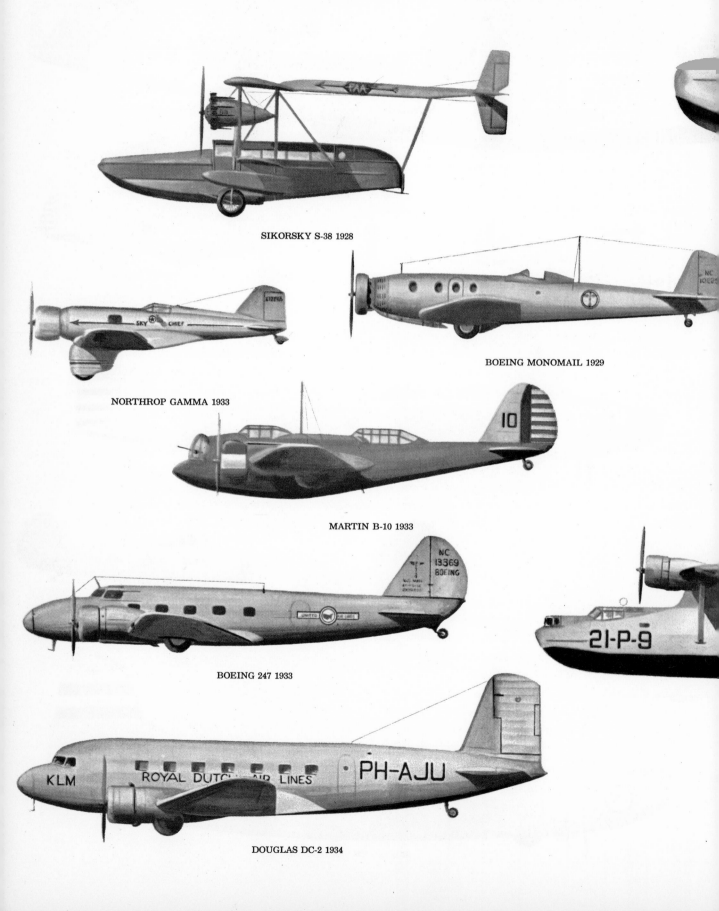

SIKORSKY S-38 1928

NORTHROP GAMMA 1933

BOEING MONOMAIL 1929

MARTIN B-10 1933

BOEING 247 1933

DOUGLAS DC-2 1934

MARTIN TRANSPORT 130 1935

GRUMMAN F3F-2 1937

SEVERSKY P-35 1937

BOEING B-17A 1938

CONSOLIDATED PBY-1 1936

STINSON RELIANT 1938

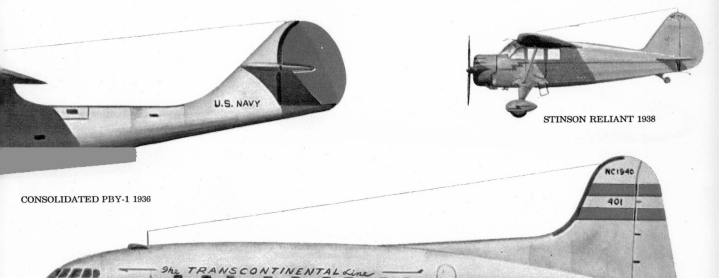

BOEING 307 STRATOLINER 1939

$2,000 in savings. But he took his idea to a group of businessmen in St. Louis, and persuaded them to raise the other $13,000 which he thought he would need to buy a long-range monoplane equipped with a Whirlwind engine. The businessmen were afraid that a single-engine plane could not make the trip, but Lindbergh replied that extra engines would simply increase the chance of engine failure. Besides, as he pointed out, they could not afford a multi-engine plane.

While Lindbergh was trying to raise the money to buy his plane, other fliers also had their eyes on the Orteig prize. A new three-engine Fokker was being built to cross the Atlantic for Commander Byrd. Two U. S. Navy lieutenants were testing a big Keystone Pathfinder biplane with three Whirlwind engines, and a French war ace, Charles Nungesser, was also planning a crossing from Europe to America.

Lindbergh knew there was no time to lose. The biggest manufacturers would not build his plane, but finally he managed to find a small California company that promised to build it, complete with engine, for only $10,580. More important, they thought they could do it in sixty days.

For two months, Lindbergh and the small company staff worked feverishly on the new plane, and exactly sixty days after the business negotiations had been settled, the plane was ready. Lindbergh called it *The Spirit of St. Louis*.

On May 10, with all the tests completed, Lindbergh flew his plane non-stop from the Pacific Coast to St. Louis in the record time of fourteen hours and twenty-five minutes. Two days later, he was in New York.

Meanwhile, things had been going badly for his rivals. Byrd's Fokker had crashed while landing and was still being repaired. The Navy lieutenants had been killed when their Keystone crashed in a marsh. And on May 8, Charles Nungesser disappeared over the Atlantic.

Lindbergh was all ready to make an attempt, but bad weather over the Atlantic held him up. For a week he was forced to wait. He spent most of the time checking and rechecking his plane and peeling off every possible ounce of weight. To reduce the weight to a minimum, he decided to fly without a radio or even a parachute.

On the night of May 19, Lindbergh had planned to go to the theater. It was raining in New York and the tops of the skyscrapers were covered with mist. But on his way to the theater, Lindbergh heard that the weather bureau was forecasting more favorable weather over the North Atlantic. Forgetting the theater, he made plans to leave early next morning.

At the moment of take-off, conditions were far from good. The runway was soaked with rain; and just as the plane was placed in position, with the wind blowing into it, the wind shifted direction and came awkwardly from behind.

But Lindbergh was sure he could get the plane off the ground, and he managed to do so, although he cleared a web of telephone wires by only twenty feet. Then he was on his way, into the misty grayness of the early morning. Almost immediately, he found himself facing unexpected problems. He had cut down the plane's weight to the bone, but during the take-off, lumps of mud and dirt had been thrown onto the wings, adding extra weight. Worse still, Lindbergh's body soon began to cry out for rest. But over Nova Scotia, he ran into squalls which buffeted the plane and shook him back into wakefulness.

As he headed out over the Atlantic, ominous cakes of ice appeared on the ocean. By his twelfth hour in the air, he was flying over Newfoundland, where he could see men on the ground looking up at him in amazement.

When Lindbergh finally put North America behind him, darkness had fallen and the plane was wreathed in fog. By shining a flashlight on the wings, he saw that some ice was forming on them. But his deadliest enemy was still sleep. To fight it off, he cupped his hands into the slipstream and directed the icy wind against his face. He stamped his feet and bounced up and down in his seat. Sometimes during the long night he had to hold his eyelids open with his thumbs.

Then it was morning and Lindbergh flew low over the turbulent ocean. Once he thought he saw land but immediately realized that the vision was a mirage. He had been in the air for more than twenty-five hours when he saw first a porpoise, then some birds, and finally some fishing boats, indicating that he was at last getting close to land.

After his ecstatic reception in Paris, Lindbergh flew on to Belgium and England. An enormous crowd met him at Croydon, May 29, 1927.

Circling low, he cut his engine and shouted to the fishermen: "Which way is Ireland?" The question was lost in the air but, as it happened, Lindbergh was exactly on course and two hours ahead of schedule. By this time, mounting excitement had driven away his desire for sleep. Eagerly, he flew on across the southern tip of Ireland and England and on across the Channel.

While he flew, the news of his flight had spread across the world and tens of thousands of people on both sides of the Atlantic were waiting tensely for word of his progress. When at last he landed in the dark at Le Bourget Airport at Paris, a huge crowd, hysterical with excitement, was waiting to greet him. Police surrounded his plane, but the spectators broke through the police cordon and surged around his plane. Some tore pieces off it as souvenirs, while others dragged Lindbergh out of his cockpit and carried him shoulder high in triumph.

CHAPTER SEVEN

Army Lieutenants Maitland and Hegenberger take off on 2,400-mile flight from California to Hawaii.

The Thirties

LINDBERGH'S achievement in crossing the Atlantic had a tremendous effect on American aviation. It seemed to prove, finally, that the airplane actually could do what the pioneers of flying had always claimed. It could cross oceans and so bring the different peoples of the world close together. It could help them to know each other better, in peace. Or it could help them to destroy each other, in war.

Within six weeks of Lindbergh's arrival in Paris, two more planes crossed the Atlantic. The first of them was flown by Clarence Chamberlin, who had hoped to win the Orteig prize. But Lindbergh had beaten him by two weeks, for Chamberlin did not make his flight until June 4. It turned out to be another record breaker. Accompanied by a passenger, Chamberlin flew 3,911 miles non-stop, from New York to Germany.

On June 29, another man who had hoped to win the Orteig prize, Commander Richard Byrd, finally set out for Paris. He and three other crewmen made the flight in a Fokker tri-motor, the *America.* They followed the route which Lindbergh had taken but their flight turned out to be much more dangerous. For much of the distance, they had to fly through fog. At times they climbed as high as ten thousand feet and were guided only by the luminous dials on their compass. Repeatedly, Byrd noted in his log: "Impossible to navigate."

As the *America* approached the French coast, the fog briefly lifted. Then it closed in again. The fuel was running low and the fliers decided that their only chance was to make a landing on water. Dropping flares into the ocean to illuminate the darkness, they ditched their big landplane into the water just off the Normandy beach, and sadly paddled ashore in a rubber boat.

Crossing the Atlantic from Europe to the U.S.A. proved to be more difficult than the flight from east to west. Eight attempts failed and seven fliers lost their lives before the German Baron von Huenefeld and two other men finally made the crossing in 1928 by flying a Junkers monoplane from Ireland to Labrador.

In the twelve months after Lindbergh's flight, thirty-one planes set out to cross the Atlantic. Twenty fliers lost their lives in flights that failed. But disasters could not discourage the airmen who hoped to break records and become famous. While some were following Lindbergh across the Atlantic, others were attempting the formidable task of crossing the Pacific.

In June, 1927, two United States Army lieutenants took off from Oakland, California, in a Fokker tri-motor, a sister ship of the machine in which Byrd had crossed the Atlantic. Their aim was to fly the 2,400 miles to Honolulu in Hawaii. Together with their other difficulties, they faced a particularly tough problem of navigation, for if they made even a slight error in their calculations, they might miss the islands altogether.

The fliers had the help of a radio beacon, the first time the device had been used in an overseas flight. Unluckily it was not much use because the aircraft's receiver worked only part of the time. The two men also found themselves facing another, and totally unexpected, problem: they could not find any food aboard the plane. Nonetheless, they reached Honolulu in twenty-five hours and fifty minutes. And after they landed they discovered that food had indeed been put aboard the plane but had been stowed away so carefully that they couldn't find it.

In August, 1927, James Dole, a planter in Hawaii, offered the first prize ever given for a trans-oceanic air race. The flight was to be from Oakland to Wheeler Field on the island of Oahu, and the prize money totalled $35,000. The race was given the name of "Pineapple Derby." Unfortunately, unlike many previous races, it did not advance the cause of flying. There was no challenge of a great new adventure, for the flight to Hawaii had already been made. The fliers who entered the race were simply after publicity and money. And some of the sixteen planes entered were little better than home-made crates.

Two of them crashed even before they reached Oakland. Trying to prevent any more disasters, government officials inspected the remaining planes and tested the pilots and navigators. They refused to allow six planes to go on with the race.

But four of the eight planes that were allowed to start either crashed on take-off or turned back. Only two of the remaining four planes completed the flight. The others disappeared and an Air Corps plane sent out to look for them crashed into the sea. Altogether, the Pineapple Derby was a sad affair. But in the following year the Pacific was the scene of one of the most successful flights of all time.

The fliers, Squadron Leader Charles Kingsford-Smith and Flight Lieutenant Charles Ulm, were both Australians who believed that it was possible to cross the Pacific from the United States to Australia. They did not have much money but they came over to the United States and managed to buy a secondhand Fokker tri-motor for about $15,000.

Kingsford-Smith and Ulm equipped the plane with three new Wright Whirlwind engines, and then carried out some preliminary flights to see how long they could stay in the air. Remembering the disasters of the Pineapple Derby, Australian officials tried to dissuade the two men from making the flight. But Kingsford-Smith and Ulm remained unshaken.

On May 31, 1928, with two Americans on board as navigator and radio operator, they took off from Oakland and flew to Hawaii without difficulty. From there they flew another 3,000 miles through severe winds and rain to the Fiji Islands. A third and final leg of 1,762 miles brought them to Brisbane, Australia, on June 9, and the Pacific, too, had been conquered.

Eight days later, the Atlantic was back in the news. For on June 17, 1928, an American, Amelia Earheart, became the first woman to fly across it. She made that flight as a passenger, but four years later she crossed the Atlantic again, and this time she flew solo.

By 1929, trans-oceanic flights had lost much of their novelty. However, the tremendous interest they aroused made many more people think of flying as a way to travel—especially in the United States.

Before 1927, American airlines had lagged behind while European airlines pushed ahead. Assisted by money from their governments, some European lines started to spread their air routes around the globe. Dutch planes carried passengers to the Dutch East Indies. British planes flew to India and Australia. And French planes carried passengers down across Africa as far as Madagascar.

The American airlines had remained small companies which practically ignored passengers and concentrated on carrying the mail. Lindbergh's flight changed all that. In the twelve months after he crossed the Atlantic, the number of people who applied for pilot's licenses in the United States shot up from 1,800 to 5,500. And in 1928 four times as many people flew as passengers as had flown in 1927.

The planes themselves kept pace with the growing public interest. As more and more people took to flying, passenger aircraft became steadily more efficient. In 1927, the Lockheed company came out with a high-wing monoplane, the Vega, which was the first American-built transport able to rival the planes built by the Dutchman Fokker and the German Junkers. The Vega could carry a pilot and six passengers at speeds up to 135 miles per hour from 500 to 900 miles.

A Hamilton all-metal monoplane takes on freight shipments transferred from Railway to Air Express.

Other developments followed quickly. The more powerful 425-horsepower Pratt and Whitney Wasp engine was replacing the old 225-horsepower Wright Whirlwind. And in 1928 a way was found to increase speed without any increase in engine power. This was the engine cowling, a smooth, detachable metal cover which fitted over the engine and so reduced wind resistance.

Then, in 1929, the two-way radio was introduced into passenger aircraft, allowing the pilot to talk to control officers on the ground. In 1929, also, James Doolittle took off and landed a plane blind, using instruments to guide him. This was a long step forward, because it meant that pilots, using instruments, would be able to take off and land even in bad weather when they could not see clearly.

These technical advances helped to encourage commercial flights. But there was another and much more important reason why commercial aviation suddenly began to expand. Businessmen had come to realize that there was money to be made from it. One of the most far-sighted of these businessmen was Juan Trippe, who founded Pan American Airways. Trippe got his start in July of 1927, when he won a contract to carry mail between Florida and Cuba. Within three years, his company had grown so fast that its amphibious planes and flying boats were flying all around South America.

In the United States, many different companies fought a bitter struggle for control of aerial transport. By the end of the year 1930, three of them had come out on top. One, American Airlines, operated mostly in the South. Another, United Airlines, operated between the West Coast and New York. The third, Transcontinental and Western Air (TWA), also flew from coast to coast.

Because of the payments they received from the government, the airlines made more money from carrying mail than they made from carrying passengers. To change this situation, Congress passed the McNary-Watres Act. Under the old law, the airlines had been paid for the amount of mail they carried. Under the new law, they were paid according to the amount of space there was available for carrying cargo. The idea behind the new law was that the airlines would build planes with more

space, and as they would not need all the extra space for carrying mail, they would use some of it to carry passengers. The new law also tried to encourage the airlines to use better planes by providing extra payments to companies which used multi-engine planes and the latest navigational equipment.

Competition between the companies continued to grow and, trying to get ahead of its rivals, each airline kept demanding better and more efficient planes. The Boeing company was one of the leading manufacturers and, in February of 1933, it came up with a low-wing, all-metal monoplane which was in many ways the first modern airliner. This plane, the 247, could carry ten passengers. It had two radial, cowled engines but could fly on one if the other failed.

This plane might have been expected to remain superior to its competitors for many years. But within a few months an even better plane appeared, built by the Douglas company.

Donald Douglas, the founder of the company, had been passionately interested in aviation since the day in 1908 when, as a youngster, he had watched Orville Wright demonstrate his flying machine at Fort Myer. Later, he worked as Glenn Martin's chief engineer. Then, in 1921, he formed his own company behind a barber's shop in Santa Monica, California.

Since then, the Douglas company had gone through hard times. But in August, 1932, Douglas received an exciting query from Jack Frye, vice-president of TWA. Frye wanted to know if Douglas could build an all-metal, tri-motor monoplane which could carry a crew of two and at least twelve passengers at a speed of 150 miles an hour for a thousand miles.

Douglas designers promptly set to work and within a year they produced the DC (Douglas Commercial)-1, which was a big improvement over the Boeing 247. It was a three engine, all-metal monoplane, as Frye had asked, and it had a stressed skin-covering that enabled it to bear great weight. It was slightly larger than the Boeing 247 and slightly faster.

The DC-1 cost $307,000 to develop and produce, but only one was ever built. It passed all its tests so successfully that TWA ordered twenty-five of the planes. But TWA officials also asked for certain changes to be made, and these changes were incorporated in a slightly different model, which was called the DC-2.

Between them, the DC-1 and the DC-2 included at least two new and extremely important improvements. One was the variable-pitch propeller. The old style, fixed-pitch propeller had always faced the wind head-on. Variable pitch meant that the propeller could be turned from head-on to edge-on, and so could bite into the wind at different angles. The effect of turning the propeller edge-on was to hold the plane back rather than to propel it forward, and so the variable pitch adjustment was particularly valuable when landing.

The DC-1/DC-2 was also equipped with flaps. They were extra sections—or trailing edges—on the backs of the wings, close to the fuselage, which could be raised or lowered. Lowering the flaps had two effects. It produced more lift at low speeds and it increased the amount of drag, thus acting as a brake. For both reasons, lowering the flaps enabled planes to land safely at lower speeds.

In October, 1934, the Boeing 247 and the DC-2 both competed in an international race and did so well that the whole world was able to see what excellent planes they were. The race was from England to Australia, a distance of 11,000 miles. It was won by a British military plane, a two-engine de Havilland Comet which flew the last two and a half hours of its run on one engine. But the big American transport planes were right behind it. The DC-2 came second and the Boeing 247 third, with another Comet racer fourth.

Meanwhile, American Airlines had started a cross-country service in which passengers could sleep as they flew from coast to coast. At first the airline used Curtiss biplanes, but though the planes were reliable, they were too slow. What American Airlines really needed was a plane that could leave New York at sundown, fly through the night with two or three stops to refuel, and land in California the following day.

The airline asked Douglas if he could build such a plane. At first his engineers tried to enlarge the DC-2 and make it big enough to hold beds for overnight passengers. But in the end, they came up with a new plane, the DC-3. It was powered by

City of Los Angeles *ready for its inaugural flight with Charles Lindbergh at the controls.*

two nine-hundred-horsepower engines and was big enough to carry twenty-one passengers by day or fourteen sleeping passengers at night.

The DC-3 turned out to be the most successful transport plane ever built. For one thing, it was extremely strong and durable. The planes wore so well that some of them flew as many as seventy thousand hours without having to be rebuilt.

The DC-3 was also very economical. Because each plane could carry more passengers than any other transport, it was able to earn more money. This combination of strength, speed, and economy made the DC-3 enormously popular. The Douglas company built something over two hundred DC-2's. It built almost eleven thousand DC-3's and some of them were still flying as late as the 1960's. By then, DC-3's had carried approximately 600,000,000 passengers.

The growing popularity of passenger flying soon brought a completely new kind of job into existence. It was born when a girl named Ellen Church decided that she would like to combine her training as a nurse and her love of flying in the same job. In 1930 she suggested the idea of air stewardess to the Boeing company and was promptly hired.

Ellen Church (at right) and early hostesses

Being an air stewardess, as Ellen Church has recalled, was a lot more difficult in the 1930's than it is today. For one thing, the stewardesses had to look after sick passengers, and airsickness was then much more common. The stewardesses also had to do some heavy carrying and fetching. Sometimes, as Ellen Church remembers, a plane

would land at an emergency landing field and fuel would be brought out in two-and-a-half- or five-gallon cans. Everyone available, including passengers and the stewardess, would then form a line and pass the cans from hand to hand until they reached the plane. When the plane was ready to start, the engines had to be adjusted. And if there were no spare crew men available, it was the stewardess who had to venture out along the wing to fix the engine.

With each year that passed, more and more people took to flying, overseas as well as at home. One line, Pan American, concentrated on overseas flights and gradually pushed its routes across the Pacific. On November 22, 1935, the famous *China Clipper* set out from California on its first commercial flight to the Philippines. By 1937, the route was extended to Hong Kong and so linked the United States to the mainland of Asia, more than 8,500 miles away.

But it was at home that commercial flying grew fastest. In 1926 the United States domestic air-

Pan American's famous China Clipper *flies over the Golden Gate bridge on its way to the Orient.*

lines had carried six thousand people. Fifteen years later they were carrying about three million people a year.

While the airlines were turning flying into a part of everyday life, daring pilots were continuing to break records. Among the most famous was a one-eyed ex-parachute jumper named Wiley Post. He became famous in 1931 when, accompanied by a navigator, he flew his Lockheed Vega, the *Winnie Mae*, around the world in eight days, fifteen hours, and fifty-one minutes.

Two years later, in July of 1933, Post tried again. In the previous year, the Sperry Gyroscope Company had perfected the automatic pilot. This was a device which could control a plane automatically on a fixed course, and so allow the pilot to snatch periods of rest. With the aid of an automatic pilot, Wiley Post made a trip around the world solo. He made the flight in seven days and nineteen hours, cutting almost a whole day off his previous time. This round-the-world trip was one of the most extraordinary feats of endurance in flying history. Two years later, when flying with the famous comedian Will Rogers, Post crashed in Alaska, and both he and Rogers were killed.

Still the records kept being broken. Two months after the death of Wiley Post, a tall Texas millionaire named Howard Hughes set a new record for landplanes by flying at 325 miles per hour. Three years later, Hughes and four companions made a round-the-world flight. The plane was a Lockheed 14 and it was so full of new gadgets that it was like a flying laboratory. It was powered by two Wright Cyclone engines, and Hughes took it round the world in the astonishingly short time of three days, nineteen hours, and fourteen minutes.

Hughes, like Lindbergh, was modest about his great achievement. "Please remember," he said, "that I am but one of five persons who made that trip, and being taller than any of them kept getting in the way and making a nuisance of myself. If you must praise anyone, save your shouts for Wiley Post." Both Wiley Post and Howard Hughes had flown around the world by taking the relatively short route across the Arctic Circle. In 1937, Amelia Earhart decided to fly around the world also, but she chose the much longer 27,000-mile route close to the equator.

Wiley Post climbing out of the Winnie Mae *after his solo flight around the world in 1933.*

Before setting off, Amelia Earhart announced that this would be her last long-distance flight. She made it in a Lockheed Electra, accompanied by a navigator named Fred Noonan. Late in June, they reached New Guinea in the Southwest Pacific. The next place they were supposed to stop was tiny Howard Island, 2,556 miles away across the South Pacific. Noonan had trouble setting his chronometers accurately, and he was worried about them. However, they took off on July 2. A U. S. Coast Guard vessel, the *Itasca*, was stationed near Howard Island. It received messages from the plane which reported head winds and stated that a great deal of gasoline was being used. Then the ship received one last, fragmentary call that seemed to indicate the Electra was off course and lost. After that there was silence. The plane was never seen again and its disappearance is still a mystery.

While one set of pilots was blazing new trails around the world, another group was concentrating on short distances. Every year, huge crowds packed the stands to watch air races. Two prizes were competed for with special eagerness. One was the Thompson Trophy, given for the fastest speed in a race over a closed course. The other was the Bendix Trophy, awarded to the winner of a coast-to-coast race across the continent.

Year after year, new records were established, only to be quickly broken. "Records of today," said the famous racing pilot Frank Hawks, "are the commonplaces of tomorrow." Hawks' own experiences were a good example. He got his flying training as an Army pilot and barnstormer, and in 1929 he flew from California to New York in a record-breaking eighteen hours and twenty-one minutes. In 1931, he flew from Los Angeles to New York in twelve and a half hours. But in 1937, Howard Hughes cut the record down to seven and a half hours.

It was the same over short distances. In 1929, Douglas Davis won the Thompson Trophy by flying at 194 miles per hour. In 1930, the winning speed was 201 miles an hour. In 1932, James Doolittle raced around the ten-lap, ten-mile course in a barrel-like plane called the Granville Gee Bee at a record 252 miles per hour. And in 1938, Roscoe Turner, the only man to win the Thompson Trophy three times, went around at 283 miles an hour.

Throughout the 1930's, flying of all kinds—for business and travel and sport—became steadily safer. But there was one exception: the dirigible. From the late twenties on, dirigibles suffered a series of terrible disasters.

In 1928, on his way back from a flight to the North Pole, the Italian General Umberto Nobile crashed his dirigible, the *Italia,* on an ice pack. The crew were able to send out a faint distress signal and tremendous efforts were made to rescue them. During the search the famous explorer Roald Amundsen disappeared. But in the end the survivors were picked up, some by airplanes, others by a Russian icebreaker.

This accident was followed by several much more dreadful disasters. In 1930, the British dirigible R-101 crashed in flames in France, and only six out of the 54 people aboard survived. The British thereupon gave up flying dirigibles, but the United States and Germany carried on.

In 1933, the American-built airship the *Akron* crashed at sea in a storm off the New Jersey coast, and 73 out of 76 crewmen were lost. And two years later, the *Akron's* sister-ship, the *Macon,* was wrecked off the California coast.

Despite all these disasters, many people continued to have confidence in the great airships, and preferred to travel in them rather than in airplanes. One reason perhaps was that some dirigibles were extremely luxurious. The biggest

of them, the German *Hindenburg,* had a cabin for every one of its 72 passengers, with hot and cold water, heating and air conditioning. It had a dining room, a lounge and a promenade. There were four cooks aboard, and a piano for concerts, and passengers could make telephone calls to Europe or America while they were in flight.

But it was the mighty *Hindenburg* that brought dirigible flights to an end. On the evening of May 6, 1937, it was coming in to land at Lakehurst, New Jersey. It came down to less than 200 feet. Then, suddenly, disaster struck. Flames started to rage at the upper section of the rear, and in a few seconds the whole tail area was aflame.

Thirty-six people were killed in the crash and many of the survivors were badly burned. Germany was the last country to fly dirigibles and, after the *Hindenburg* disaster, the German dictator, Adolf Hitler, ordered all other dirigibles to be grounded. They never flew again. The age of the dirigible had come to an end.

But every year the airplane was becoming more important, in war as well as in peace. As far back as 1921, an Italian officer named Guilio Douhet had insisted that future wars would be won by air forces. His theory was that airplanes should be used to carry out mass raids on enemy cities. Such raids, Douhet believed, could destroy the will of a people to keep fighting.

His theories were studied by military leaders all over the world. They were first tested in action by the Italian dictator, Benito Mussolini. In 1935, Mussolini ordered Italian troops to invade the primitive African country of Ethiopia. More than three hundred combat planes were thrown into the attack, most of them three-engine bombers. They faced almost no opposition and were able to bomb the Ethiopian cities as they wished. They even used poison gas, which Douhet had said was more effective than ordinary explosive bombs.

In the following year, Mussolini had another chance to test his air force, this time in Spain. A group of rebels led by General Francisco Franco, rose in rebellion against the Spanish government, and Mussolini took Franco's side. For three years the war raged in Spain. In that time, more than seven hundred Italian planes carried out some five thousand bombing missions.

One of the worst disasters in aviation history. The Hindenburg *bursts into flames as it is about to land at Lakehurst, New Jersey. This brought the age of dirigibles to an end.*

The Italians were not the only outsiders to intervene in Spain. Adolf Hitler was also eager to try out his air force in combat and he, too, decided to help Franco. In August, 1936, the Germans gave Franco six fighters and twenty bomber-transports. In November, they started to send fliers to Spain disguised as tourists. But once in Spain, the "tourists" formed up into a miniature air force which was called the Condor Legion.

The Germans concentrated particularly on two kinds of combat planes. One was the fighter, used to machine-gun enemy troops from a low level. The other was the Junkers 87-A (Stuka) dive bomber. When they reached their target, the Stukas would go into a steep dive and drop their bombs from a few feet above the ground.

These Stukas were slow. They could be shot down quite easily by enemy fighters or by experienced ground troops. But to soldiers who were not used to them they were terrifying.

At the same time another war was raging in the Far East, where the Japanese were invading China. The Japanese were far the stronger, especially in the air, and they launched bombers on raids against Chinese cities. These bombers were protected by fighters which became known as Zeros. They were light, maneuverable and heavily armed, and so much better than any Chinese planes that the weak Chinese air force was practically driven out of the skies.

While the Italians, the Germans, and the Japanese were all developing their air forces, and test-ing them in battle, the western countries were making little effort to build up their air power. In 1938, for example, the Germans had 1,200 bombers ready for battle. To oppose them, the British had exactly 46 fighters.

The United States, too, had made little effort to prepare its air force for a major war. Its leaders were quite sure that the United States would never start a war by attacking another country. They therefore assumed that airplanes would be needed only to defend the country against an attack from some enemy.

In such a war, as the military leaders saw it, the Navy would be the first line of defense. In addition, land-based bombers would be used to fly out to sea and sink the invader's ships. The U. S. Army Air Corps therefore concentrated on building bombers.

One of them was the most powerful bomber in the world. It was a four-engine long-range bomber designed by Boeing which was first known as the XB-17. When it was tested in August, 1935, it flew 2,100 miles non-stop at an average speed of 232 miles per hour, a performance that no other plane in the world could equal.

Toward the end of the 1930's, the United States began to quicken its preparations for war. The number of Navy planes had been around a thousand. But in May, 1938, Congress gave the Navy permission to triple the number. Then, in September, 1938, President Roosevelt called for the Army Air Corps to be enlarged to 10,000 planes.

The explanation of these quickened preparations was that the danger of war was increasing rapidly. The main threat came from Adolf Hitler, who had openly admitted that he planned to conquer much of Europe. To back up his threats, Hitler was building up his army and air force at top speed.

Just in time, the British, like the Americans, began to build up their air power. By 1939, the British had more than five hundred fighters ready. The French, too, were desperately ordering warplanes from abroad. But before they could receive any large deliveries of planes, the threatened war had broken out. On September 1, 1939, Hitler sent his tanks racing into Poland, while above them, 1,600 German warplanes struck at the Polish army and air force. World War II had begun.

A group of Boeing P-26's, the U.S. Army's first all-metal pursuit plane and monoplane fighter

CHAPTER EIGHT

British R.A.F. pilots race toward their Spit-fires. Many had to fly several missions each day.

World War II

THE German air force, the Luftwaffe, opened its attack on Poland by launching a storm of bombs on Polish airfields. Within two days, German bombers and fighters had cut the Polish air force to pieces. Most of the Polish planes were destroyed on the ground.

In ten days of fighting, the Polish army, too, was practically destroyed. Soon afterwards, the Russians invaded Poland from the east and, within a month, the whole country was occupied by Germany and Russia.

Britain and France had promised to come to Poland's aid. As soon as she was attacked, they declared war on Germany. But neither the British nor the French made any strong attempt to attack Germany, and throughout the winter, the frontier between France and Germany remained almost peaceful. It was so quiet that it was described as the "phony war."

In the spring of 1940, Hitler struck again. On April 9, he attacked both Denmark and Norway. To get at Norway, the Germans had to cross the dividing sea. In addition to ships, they used nearly three hundred planes to lift soldiers into Norway, and these troops rapidly seized Norway's main ports and airfields. The British Royal Air Force could not operate in daylight so far from its own bases, and so the Luftwaffe was easily able to keep control of the air. Within a few days Norway was conquered.

Since 1937 Britain's prime minister had been Neville Chamberlain. The British people were dissatisfied with the "phony war" and many of them blamed Chamberlain for the failure to save Norway from the German attack. On May 10, 1940, he was replaced as prime minister by Winston Churchill.

That same day, the quiet along Germany's western frontier was abruptly shattered by a German invasion of Holland, Belgium, and Luxembourg. It was probably the most violent invasion in history. Tanks stormed across the frontiers by the hundreds while Stuka dive bombers screamed down on the defenders. Behind the front lines, German parachutists, many of them in disguise, seized bridges and road crossings and in general created confusion.

The German attack was irresistible. On May 15, after four and a half days of fighting, the Dutch surrendered. Twelve days later, the Belgians surrendered also. Several hundreds of thousands of British troops had advanced to help the Belgians, and the Belgian surrender left them in danger of being surrounded. But they managed to reach the French coast at Dunkirk before the Germans.

There they waited in long lines on the beaches while the British collected every available seaworthy craft to cross the Channel and bring them home. As the little ships ferried soldiers off the beaches, German bombers pounded them mercilessly. However, Royal Air Force planes, flying from bases in England, managed to hold most of the German bombers off. And many of the bombs that were dropped exploded harmlessly in the sand. Altogether more than 350,000 Allied troops were taken off the beaches and carried across the Channel to safety.

A German Dornier bomber, range 900 miles, crossing the Channel on its way to raid Britain.

Still the German attack continued. German tanks had split the French defenses wide open and every day the Germans cut deeper into the heart of France. On June 10, Hitler's ally, Mussolini, declared war on France and attacked from the south. On June 20, the French surrendered, and next day an armistice was signed at Compiègne, where the Germans had surrendered twenty years earlier to end World War I.

Britain now stood alone. But she was separated from Europe by the English Channel, and the question was whether Hitler would attempt to send his army across the water. The Germans had not prepared any plans for an invasion and they had no boats ready to ferry troops. Hitler hinted that he was ready to make a peace settlement. But Prime Minister Churchill refused to consider making peace. If he wanted to end the war, Hitler had to crush Britain.

The German army was overwhelmingly stronger than the British army, but the British navy was overwhelmingly stronger than the German navy. If the Germans wanted to launch a successful invasion, they would have to keep the British navy from sinking the invasion ships. That meant they had to drive the British warships out of the Channel. They could do so by bombing but first they had to protect their bombers against attacks from the British. Thus, in order to launch an invasion, the Germans had to destroy the Royal Air Force's fighters and so win control of the air.

The commander-in-chief of the Luftwaffe, Hermann Goering, had approximately 930 fighters and nearly 1,300 bombers ready for the battle. To meet this force, the British had less than 700 fighters, most of them Hurricanes and Spitfires.

The battle between the German and British air forces for control of the skies over the English Channel and southern England has become known as the Battle of Britain. It opened early in July when the Germans began to bomb Britain's ships and ports. Their plan was to lure the RAF's fighters up into battle where they could be shot down. But the British understood the plan, and held their planes back to wait for the heavier attacks which they knew would soon begin.

From August 8, the German attacks grew heavier. Now the main targets were the airfields and radar stations along Britain's south and east coasts. The radar stations consisted of approximately twenty electronic spotters which could "pick up" enemy planes when they were still several miles away and before they could be seen. In addition, the radar indicated how many planes there were, their height, and the direction in which they were flying.

By August 13, the German attack was reaching its peak. On that day, the Luftwaffe flew 1,485 sorties and lost 47 planes. RAF fighters flew 700 sorties and lost 13 planes. The next day was quieter. The Germans lost 19 planes and the British eight.

But August 15 was the most violent day yet. German planes made 1,786 sorties, the largest number made by either side on any one day of the battle. During the day, British officers who were keeping track of the fighting became increasingly worried as they observed that there were always more attackers than defenders. But although it had far more planes in the air, the Luftwaffe did not succeed in breaking through the British defenses. The British claimed that they had shot down 182 planes while the Germans claimed that they had shot down 134 British planes. After the war, it was found that these claims were greatly exaggerated.

Meanwhile the Germans had been seriously misled. They thought the British possessed at least three times as many fighters as they actually had.

Trapped on the surface, the crew of a German U-boat waits helplessly as a British Hudson circles above.

This was because the Germans did not have any radar of their own, and they did not know about the radar stations which enabled the British to see where the next attack was coming from and direct their fighters to meet it. The British, but not the Germans, also had ground-to-air radio communications. This meant that officers could direct planes already in the air to shift direction and go to where they were most urgently needed.

For a few days there was a lull in the fighting because of bad weather. But on August 24, the Germans returned to the attack. They had now decided to make fewer but heavier attacks and sent their bombers over in groups of up to forty. Each group was escorted by more than a hundred fighters whose job was to hold off the British Hurricanes and Spitfires.

The Germans concentrated their new blows on two targets: the fighter airfields and the command posts of Britain's fighter defense. The massive attacks badly damaged the British fighter organization, and the defenders lost more planes than they could replace. In two weeks, the British lost 277 aircraft to the Germans' 378. Even more serious, 230 British pilots, a quarter of their total number, were either killed or wounded.

If the Germans, with their superior numbers, had continued to use the same tactics, the British fighters would have been swept from the skies. But just as he was nearing victory, the German commander, Hermann Goering, changed his plans.

The reason for the change was completely accidental. On the night of August 24, German planes made a mistake in navigation and accidentally dropped their bombs on central London. But Prime Minister Churchill naturally assumed that the attack had been deliberately aimed at London, and he suggested that the RAF should pay the Germans back by bombing Berlin.

Goering had boasted that Berlin would never be bombed. But on August 25 it was bombed, by 81 British planes. On the following night, it was attacked again. Hitler was enraged by these raids and he determined to revenge them by destroying the cities of Britain.

On September 3, Goering held a conference with two of his top commanders, Hugo Sperrle and Albert Kesselring, to discuss the change of plan.

Sperrle believed that the British still had plenty of fighters left and thought the Luftwaffe should continue its attacks against the airfields. Kesselring thought the RAF was beaten. Goering believed that the British were pulling their fighters back, out of range of German attacks. Only if London were bombed, said Goering, would the British risk their last fighter reserves. It was two against one, and the switch to attacks on London was ordered.

Huge areas of the city were wiped out. But though the Luftwaffe was able to wreck large parts of Britain's capital, it had failed to carry out its main aim. It had not been able to win control of the skies over the Channel and southern England. Because of that failure, the Germans were not able to invade Britain. In September, Hitler put off his plan to invade Britain until October. In October, he put it off until the following year. But actually the plan was dead. The Germans had suffered their first defeat. The British had proved that the Luftwaffe could be overcome and they had also proved that Germany itself was open to attack.

One reason for the German failure in the Battle of Britain was that the German commanders had not really learned how to use their air power. They understood very well how airplanes could help their army in battle. But they did not know how to make the best use of an air force operating on its own.

The British had not been able to concentrate all their resources on the Battle of Britain. While they were holding off the Luftwaffe at home, they were also fighting in the Mediterranean and in Africa. Here, the enemy was the Italians who, in September, 1940, had launched attacks from their African colonies against the British territory of Kenya and the British-occupied country of Egypt.

The shortest supply routes to Africa lay across the Mediterranean, and both the British and the Italians were anxious to control this vital sea. The advantage seemed to lie with the Italians. For the British had to keep so many ships in the Atlantic to resist possible German attacks that the Italians were left with superior forces in the Mediterranean. But on November 11, 1940, the position was abruptly altered. Torpedo-carrying

A German Ju-87 Stuka dive bomber, shown in typical, almost vertical, dive in a raid on Warsaw.

planes from the British fleet attacked the Italian fleet in its harbor at Taranto and put half of the most powerful ships in the fleet out of action.

Then, in December, 1940, the small British army in Egypt attacked the Italians and drove them back hundreds of miles across Libya. In this campaign, the British took about 130,000 Italian prisoners.

The Germans were a much more formidable enemy. In the spring of 1941, they invaded first Yugoslavia and then Greece. Almost a thousand planes of the Luftwaffe took part in the offensives. The British sent a small force across the Mediterranean into Greece, but though they fought desperately they were unable to hold the Germans back for more than a few days. By that time, they had only twenty-four planes left out of the nine squadrons they had sent into Greece. And just as they had done at Dunkirk, the British had to ferry their defeated army out by sea, this time to the island of Crete in the eastern Mediterranean.

British warships controlled the waters around Crete and kept the Germans from invading it by sea. But the Germans controlled the skies, and Crete became the scene of the first attack in history to be carried out entirely from the air. On May 20, the German Eleventh Air Corps struck at the island. First, the Germans dropped parachutists to seize and hold landing strips. Then they flew troops into the island in transports and gliders. More than five hundred Junkers-52 transports and one hundred gliders took part in the operation.

The defenders, mostly New Zealanders, fought fiercely, but the Germans were too strong for them. Once again the British navy had to ferry a defeated army away from the battlefield and, as it was carrying the troops back to North Africa, it lost several ships to German dive-bombing.

The Germans pressed their advantage by placing large numbers of bombers on the island of Sicily. These bombers made it terribly difficult for British ships to operate in the central Mediterranean. Shielded by their air force, German transport ships were able to carry troops and supplies across the Mediterranean to Libya. There, the Germans built up an army which became known as the Afrika Corps. Faced with the superior strength of this army, the British had to retreat back into Egypt.

On June 22, 1941, Hitler turned on Germany's traditional enemy, Russia. With the assistance of Finns, Hungarians, and Rumanians, and spearheaded by 2,770 planes of the Luftwaffe, the German army smashed across the thousand-mile frontier. As usual, the Germans scored rapid successes. During the opening offensive Russian planes were spotted standing on unprotected airfields and were destroyed by the hundreds. Some Russian planes did manage to get into the sky but they were routed by the battle-hardened German pilots. With the air cleared of enemy fighters, the Stuka dive bombers were once again allowed free play, and one renowned dive-bomber pilot, Hans Rudel, is believed to have destroyed more than five hundred Russian tanks.

By the end of 1941, the Nazi armies had advanced enormous distances into Russian territory. Altogether, on the ground and in the air, the Germans had destroyed more than eight thousand Russian planes. But far beyond the front lines, out of reach of Germany's two-engine bombers, new Russian war plants were beginning to turn out planes. As the new year began, the Russian air force started to recover.

Early on December 7, 1941, a powerful force of Japanese aircraft carriers, which had left Japan secretly on November 28, reached a point about two hundred miles north of the Hawaiian Islands. At dawn, with the crews of the ships cheering them off, a first wave of 183 Japanese planes set off for a surprise attack on the great American naval base at Pearl Harbor. Their mission was to smash the American air defenses. The commanders at Pearl Harbor had not prepared themselves and the surprise was complete.

The first wave of raiders struck at 7:55 in the morning. They concentrated on destroying American planes that were standing on the ground, in order to leave the air free for the waves of bombers and torpedo planes that were coming after them. Only twenty-five planes managed to get into the air and four of them were shot down.

Then came the main attack—from 170 Japanese planes. With practically no interference from American planes, they bombed and torpedoed the American fleet lying at anchor in the harbor. There were eight American battleships in the harbor; every one of them was either sunk or damaged. By nine o'clock the raid was over and the Japanese had gone. They had lost 29 planes and 55 men. In return, they had killed more than 2,000 Americans and practically destroyed the United States Pacific fleet.

The United States also had bases on the Philippine Islands, and there very much the same thing happened. Although the American commanders had been warned to guard against possible attack, they took no precautions. With almost no opposition, Japanese planes, flying in from carriers, shot up the airfields and destroyed row upon row of American planes on the ground.

The British were the next to suffer from the Japanese aerial onslaught. On December 10, 1941, two of the most powerful ships in the British Navy, the *Prince of Wales* and the *Repulse,* were steaming north in the Gulf of Siam. Hurrying north to cut off a Japanese convoy that was landing troops in Malaya, they had sailed beyond the range of fighter protection. The British admiral had relied on the low clouds to conceal his ships from the Japanese. But unluckily, the clouds cleared, the ships were spotted, and land-based torpedo bombers were sent out to attack them.

With the loss of only three planes, shot down by anti-aircraft fire, the bombers sank both the mighty ships. This loss shattered British naval power in the Pacific. "In all the war," Winston Churchill wrote later, "I never received a more direct shock."

This aerial attack finally proved that General Billy Mitchell had been right back in the 1920's. In a fight between bombers and ships, the bombers were almost bound to win. Unless it was protected by friendly aircraft, no ship could survive determined attack from the air.

The Japanese now had control of the seas in the western Pacific, and their forces rapidly swept outwards. They captured the British bases and colonies of Hong Kong, Singapore, Malaya, and Burma. They occupied the Dutch East Indies. They cut China off from her allies and left her isolated. American troops, assisted by a handful of Marine

Japanese bombers sinking the British battleship
Prince of Wales *and the battle cruiser* Repulse

Wildcat planes, did manage to fight off a Japanese attack against tiny Wake Island. But ten days later, the Japanese sent in a larger force and captured the island.

With their sea and air power in the western Pacific destroyed, the United States was helpless to stop the Japanese advances. But at last, in April, 1942, the Americans did get their first slight taste of revenge. It came in the form of a raid on Tokyo, the capital of Japan, launched from the carrier *Hornet.*

The bold raid did not do much damage to Tokyo, but it did worry the Japanese and it led them to divert some of their air force to defending their home islands. It also gave a boost to American confidence, which had been damaged by the succession of Japanese victories.

The Japanese were soon to suffer a much more important setback. Early in May, a B-17 spotted a Japanese troop-carrying convoy sailing south across the Coral Sea toward the Allied base of Port Moresby on the island of New Guinea. An American fleet moved to intercept it, and for two days a confused battle raged between the two groups of carrier-based planes.

The Battle of the Coral Sea was the first naval clash in history in which the opposing ships never came into contact with each other. All the attacking was done by the airplanes. The American planes sank one Japanese carrier and damaged another. The Japanese achieved the same results; they sank the carrier *Lexington* and damaged the *Yorktown.* But though both sides suffered about the same losses, the battle really amounted to an American victory, for the Japanese invasion fleet was forced to turn back.

This setback did not keep the Japanese from pressing forward elsewhere. Early in June, they sent a fleet into the central Pacific, intending to capture Midway Island and establish bases in the Aleutians. To carry out these attacks, Japanese

Admiral Isoroku Yamamoto assembled a huge striking force of more than 150 ships, which included battleships, cruisers, destroyers, submarines, and carriers with about 1,000 planes aboard.

The Japanese hoped that their attack would force the remnants of the U. S. Pacific fleet into action, and so give them a chance to destroy the remaining American ships in one final, decisive battle. But Admiral Yamamoto made two serious blunders. First, he divided his air strength by sending two carriers north to help his force in the Aleutian islands. Second, he was late in spotting two American task forces, commanded by Admirals Raymond A. Spruance and Frank J. Fletcher, that were racing toward Midway.

For the Americans had set an ambush. They had broken Japan's naval code, and they knew from intercepted messages that the Japanese were coming. As the Japanese fleet approached Midway, an American force of three carriers waited on its flank.

On June 4, Japanese planes attacked Midway and shattered its defenses. In return, bombers from Midway and Devastator planes from the lurking carriers attacked the Japanese fleet. They were driven off, and 35 out of 41 Devastators were shot down.

It looked as though the Japanese were about to win another smashing victory. Then suddenly, the ambush worked. Another group of planes left the waiting American carriers, and this time they were Dauntless dive bombers. Sweeping down at a slanting 70-degree angle from 17,000 to 2,500 feet, they took the Japanese completely by surprise. In five minutes, their bombs sank three Japanese carriers. Later in the battle, the Japanese lost another carrier and a cruiser.

The Japanese sank the carrier *Yorktown*. But there was no doubt who had won the Battle of Midway. The Dauntless dive bombers had transformed it from an American defeat into a tremendous success. The Japanese never recovered from the loss of the combat fliers and technicians who went down with their carriers. Yamamoto sent back a message, stating: "Occupation of Midway is canceled." The message also had a deeper significance. It marked the point at which the Japanese sweep across the Pacific was halted, never to be resumed.

Douglas SBD Dauntless dive bombers race in to surprise Japanese fleet at the Battle of Midway.

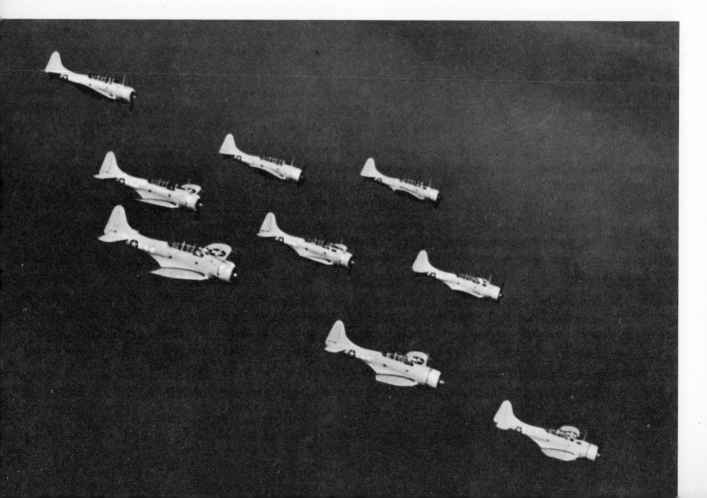

CHAPTER NINE

With its five-inch rockets blazing, an F4U Corsair rakes Japanese hill positions on Okinawa.

Allied Triumph

THE Japanese attack on Pearl Harbor had brought the United States into the war against Germany and Italy as well as against Japan. At the outset, the American leaders made a vital decision. They decided to throw most of their resources into the battle against Germany in order to end the war in Europe as quickly as possible. Then, when Germany was defeated, they would turn their full strength against the Japanese.

To defeat Germany, it was necessary to invade Europe. The Allies planned to launch the invasion across the English Channel against northern France. The main task of the air forces would be to assist the invasion. But in 1942 the Allies were not ready to invade Europe, and the British and American governments agreed that the best use they could make of their air power was to weaken the Germans by heavy bombing.

Early in June of 1942, Major General Carl Spaatz of the U. S. Army Air Corps arrived in England to take command of the American Eighth Air Force. From the beginning, he and the other American air commanders disagreed with the British about the best way to carry out the bombing offensive against Germany.

The British, like the Germans, had tried daylight bombing. But they lost so many planes in day raids that they had turned to night bombing instead. Moreover, the British did not think it was possible to hit specific targets such as war factories. They thought it was better to wipe out whole areas, acre by acre, destroying the war plants in the process.

The Americans disagreed on both points. They believed their bombers could carry out daylight raids without losing too many planes. For they had two heavy bombers, the B-17 Flying Fortress and the B-24 Liberator, which could fly fast and cover long distances. These planes carried ten or more machine guns each. Flying in close formation, the Americans hoped, the bombers would be able to fight off attackers. Secondly, the Americans believed in attacking specific targets. They had a new and much improved bombsight which, they hoped, would enable the bombers to hit individual targets with great accuracy.

For a while after the United States entered the war the British continued to do most of the bombing. Throughout 1942, the striking power of Britain's Bomber Command kept increasing. New Halifax and Lancaster bombers replaced the slower and smaller planes, and the weight of single bombs rose from two to eight thousand pounds.

In January, 1942, the British could only afford to send an average of 42 planes on each bombing mission. By December, the number was up to 261. Moreover, the planes had been equipped with radar, which meant that the pilots no longer had to rely on their eyes to locate targets. As radar worked in both good weather and bad, pilots were able to find their way to their targets in cloudy weather and on moonless nights.

Germany's great industrial center, the Ruhr, was one of the first areas to feel the RAF's new strength. On May 30, a thousand bombers attacked the city of Cologne. Using its new and longer-range planes, the RAF was also able to attack the industrial cities of northern Italy, such as Turin. It was the first city to suffer a full-scale attack made with eight-thousand-pound bombs.

Famous Airplanes: 1939-1945

MESSERSCHMITT ME-109E (GER.) 1939

SUPERMARINE SPITFIRE (BR.) 1939

HEINKEL HE-111P (GER.) 1939

AVRO LANCASTER B (BR.) 1941

CURTISS P-40E (U.S.) 1941

MARTIN B-26B (U.S.) 1942

CONSOLIDATED B-24J LIBERATOR (U.S.) 1943

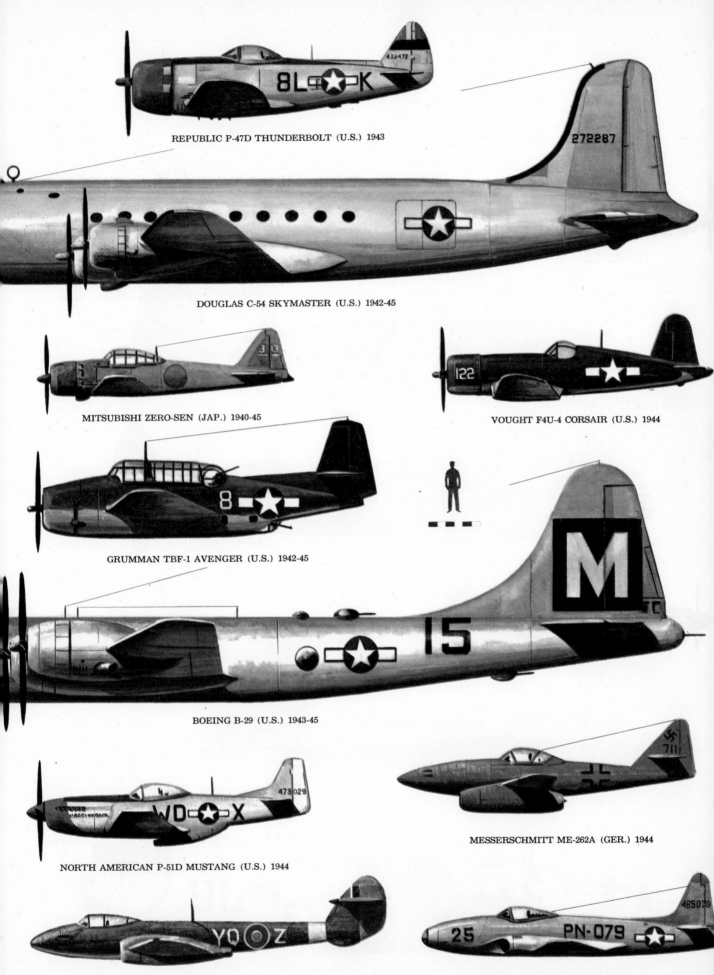

REPUBLIC P-47D THUNDERBOLT (U.S.) 1943

DOUGLAS C-54 SKYMASTER (U.S.) 1942-45

MITSUBISHI ZERO-SEN (JAP.) 1940-45

VOUGHT F4U-4 CORSAIR (U.S.) 1944

GRUMMAN TBF-1 AVENGER (U.S.) 1942-45

BOEING B-29 (U.S.) 1943-45

NORTH AMERICAN P-51D MUSTANG (U.S.) 1944

MESSERSCHMITT ME-262A (GER.) 1944

GLOSTER METEOR (BR.) 1943

LOCKHEED P-80 SHOOTING STAR (U.S.) 1944

British losses were severe. Often one plane out of ten failed to return; sometimes the losses were even heavier. But the Chief of the RAF Bomber Command, Sir Arthur Harris, believed that his bombers did enough damage to make the losses worth while.

In the summer of 1942, the American bomber group based in Britain—the U. S. Eighth Air Force—began to join in the bombing, using the American technique of daylight raids. On August 17, twelve Flying Fortresses, escorted by a group of Spitfires, bombed the railroad at Rouen in France. All returned safely and that seemed a good sign for the daylight bombing to come.

In the first week of September, the Eighth Air Force made ten more attacks on targets within the range of escorting fighters. Their bombing was so accurate that it looked as if planes flying in daylight would be able to land forty per cent of their bombs within a thousand-yard circle around the target. But on September 7 the bombers' luck changed. The weather turned bad and the bombing went wild. Still the losses remained low, for only two bombers failed to return out of ten separate missions.

Next day General Spaatz was ordered to give up a considerable number of his bombers. They were needed to cover a planned Allied invasion of North Africa. For some months, both the U. S. Eighth Air Force and the RAF Bomber Command were to be kept busy, protecting the Allied ships which were carrying troops and supplies to North Africa. And so, for the rest of 1942 and on into the following spring, the air onslaught against Germany practically came to a halt.

The invasion of North Africa was the third of three enormously important events which took place in November, 1942. The first was the battle of El Alamein in Egypt. It raged for twelve days and ended in overwhelming Allied success. Commanded by General Sir Bernard Montgomery, and helped throughout the battle from the air, the British smashed the German Afrika Corps and drove it in confused retreat out of Egypt.

The second decisive event was the battle of Stalingrad. Still advancing deep into Russia, the Germans had reached the Volga River at the city of Stalingrad. There, in August, their advance had

been halted in bitter fighting. Then, as the Russian winter closed in, the Russians counterattacked and managed to surround the Sixth German Army.

Throughout December and January, the Germans tried desperately to break through to their beleaguered forces. They lost nearly 500 planes in an all-out attempt to fly in the 550 tons of supplies which the encircled army needed each day. In their desperation, the Germans even used their newest four-engine bomber, the Heinkel He-177, as a transport.

But their losses were terribly high. Within a few weeks, a thousand highly trained airmen were lost. And in the end, all their efforts were wasted. Unable to break through the Russian cordon, and with their ammunition and food running low, the surrounded German troops finally surrendered in February.

The third decisive event of that November was the invasion of North Africa which started on the 8th. Two task forces sailed from England to land at the ports of Algiers and Oran, and a third sailed from the United States and landed at Casablanca. The invasion, which was commanded by General Dwight Eisenhower, caught the enemy completely by surprise. Algiers and Oran were quickly captured and within two days all French units in Morocco had surrendered.

Their next aim was to take over Tunisia, to the east. Dropping parachutists to capture important points, the Allies pressed forward. On November 28, they reached to within twenty miles of the capital, Tunis. But there, they were driven back by stronger German forces. And as the winter began to close in, the job of supplying the troops at the front became more difficult.

On February 14, the German General Rommel, commander of the Afrika Corps, who had been retreating before the British advance in Libya, joined the German forces in Tunisia. But the Allies were closing in. Their air forces had won complete control over the air, and they mercilessly bombarded enemy ports and ships to prevent supplies being sent to the enemy across the Mediterranean.

Unable to keep their men supplied by sea, the Germans took to the air. But on April 18, four squadrons of American P-40 fighters scored a particularly striking success. They caught nearly a

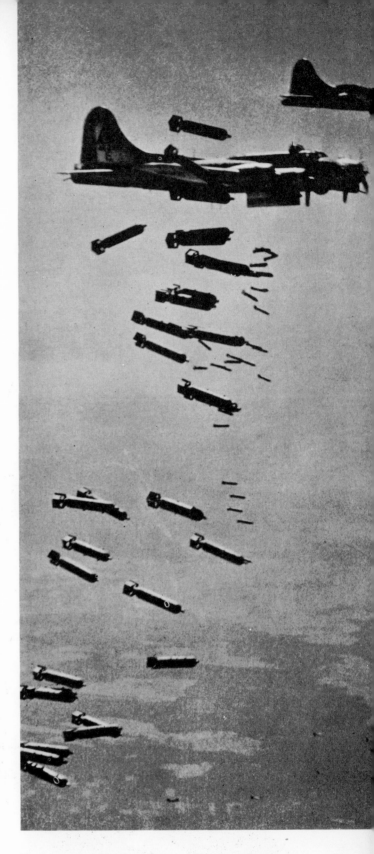

hundred big Junkers-52 transports flying with a fighter escort over the Gulf of Tunis, and shot down more than fifty of them in ten minutes.

Late in April, the Allies began their final push into Tunisia. In support of the attack, Allied planes flew more than two thousand sorties a day. The Germans and Italians were completely cut off from help because the Allies controlled both the sea and the air above it. On May 13, the entire German and Italian force surrendered.

The Allies' next major target was the island of Sicily, near the toe of the Italian boot. The Allied commanders wanted to capture air bases close to Sicily so that fighters could give the invasion troops aerial protection. The most suitable place for such bases was the tiny island of Pantelleria. It was attacked so violently from the air that the German garrison surrendered before any Allied troops even landed. This was the first time in history that any territory had been conquered by the use of air power alone.

The invasion of Sicily was planned to begin on July 10. For days beforehand, Allied planes pounded the island so heavily that they put a thousand planes and almost all its thirty-one airfields out of action. Once he had obtained complete mastery in the air, General Eisenhower sent his armada of three thousand ships toward the island. With the German air force blasted out of the sky, only a dozen ships of the Allied invasion fleet were sunk. Allied troops were able to go ashore with almost no resistance from enemy aircraft. The whole island was quickly captured and, with it, the airfields from which Allied bombers could reach targets in Italy and southern France.

While the North African campaign was being fought, most of the American Eighth Air Force had been kept busy supporting the Allied armies. Not enough planes were left in England to do much damage to Germany. But during this lull in the aerial offensive, the British and American leaders finally reached agreement on their bombing plans.

Prime Minister Churchill had been vehemently opposed to daylight bombing because he thought the losses would be too heavy. The Americans were developing long-range fighters to accompany the bombers on their missions. But though Generals Eisenhower and Spaatz tried their hardest, they could not convince Churchill that daylight bombing would be worth the losses.

Finally, General Eaker, who had taken over as commander of the Eighth Air Force, went to see Churchill. He showed the Prime Minister a paper he had drawn up stating: "If the RAF bombs by night, and we bomb by day, bombing around the clock, the German defenses will get no rest." Churchill was won over by Eaker's arguments and agreed that full-scale daylight bombing should be given a trial.

By the summer of 1943, the Eighth Air Force was at last ready to begin a really intensive bombing attack on Germany and the German-occupied countries of Europe. Germany was known to be short of oil, and so her oil supplies, particularly the huge oil refineries at Ploesti in Rumania, were chosen as especially important targets.

On August 1, 177 Liberators launched an attack on Ploesti which was supposed to come as a complete surprise to the defenders. The planes flew very low and kept radio silence. But, unluckily, the leading planes turned too soon in the direction of the target and alerted the defenses. Fifty-four of the Liberators were shot down. About forty per cent of Ploesti's refining capacity was believed to have been destroyed. But, within a few months, the refineries were working just as well as ever.

The Eighth Air Force commanders realized that the Germans were trying very hard to produce enough fighters to hold off the Allied bombers. They therefore decided to make a concentrated attack on the Messerschmitt fighter plant at the German city of Regensburg. At the same time, the Eighth Air Force planned to wipe out a factory at Schweinfurt which made ball bearings used in airplanes.

The plan was that one wave of bombers would hit Regensburg and then fly straight on across the Mediterranean to land in Algeria. Immediately afterwards, another wave would attack Schweinfurt. The idea behind this plan was that the German fighters would be so busy holding off the first wave that the attack on Schweinfurt should go through without much opposition.

On the morning of August 17, the 146 bombers due to attack Regensburg took off from their

Flying Fortress being loaded with 300-pound bombs at British base for a raid on railroad yards.

English bases. As expected, German fighters launched a series of savage attacks and twenty-four of the bombers were shot down. However, every building of the vital Messerschmitt plant was damaged, and the bombers which had survived the fighter attacks were able to fly on to Algeria without further trouble.

Unluckily, bad weather delayed the take-off of the second bomber group, headed for Schweinfurt. The Allied plan had assumed that the German fighters would be exhausted after their battles with the first bomber wave. But because of the delay, the German fighters had time to rest and refuel before the second group of bombers reached Germany, and they shot down 36 American planes.

The attack failed to destroy the vital ball-bearing plant and on October 14 the Eighth Air Force raided Schweinfurt again. This time 60 Fortresses were lost out of 291. In six October days, 148 Allied bombers were shot down. The people who had opposed daylight raids by bombers flying without fighter escort were being proved right. For without help from fighters the bombers could not protect themselves adequately against massive and determined fighter attack.

Faced with the huge bomber losses, the Allied air commanders decided to stop making daylight raids against targets deep inside Germany. Those raids were not resumed until February of 1944. By then long-range fighters were available which could escort bombers all the way.

Although the Allied bombing damaged many German factories, it had not managed to destroy them. The Germans repaired their factories very quickly after they were attacked. By the end of December, 1943, they were turning out more fighters than in the previous June.

But the raids did have one extremely useful result; they forced the Germans to keep most of their fighters in the west. When the Germans invaded Russia in 1941, they used half the Luftwaffe to help their armies. But at the end of 1943 only one German plane out of five was operating on the Russian front. The others had been pulled back to fight off the bombing attacks in the west.

Meanwhile, in the Pacific, the Allies were also gradually winning the upper hand in a series of extremely tough battles. Turned back at Midway in June, 1942, the Japanese had promptly pushed farther to the south. In July they started to drive across the island of New Guinea in the direction of Australia.

By September 17 they had reached within twenty miles of the main Allied base at Port Moresby. But American planes first knocked out the enemy's airfields and then, gradually, won control of the air. And Allied troops were airlifted from Australia into the battle zone where they began to push the Japanese back.

Japanese power began to crumble all across the Pacific. By November of 1943, Admiral Chester W. Nimitz, commander of American forces in the Central Pacific, confidently announced: "Henceforth, we propose to give the Jap no rest." The U. S. commanders stepped up their tactics of hopping from island to island, using each new one they captured as a base for attacking the next.

In the fall of 1943, for example, the Americans captured the atoll of Tarawa in the Gilbert Islands. From there, they moved on to the Marshall Islands. For several weeks Army and Navy pilots, flying off bases in the recently captured Gilberts, bombed and machine-gunned Japanese airfields in the Marshalls. Then, late in January, a Navy task force moved up and planes from its twelve carriers gained control of the air over the Marshalls.

On January 31, 1944, troops landed on Kwajalein Atoll in the Marshalls. Supported by air attacks and gunfire from ships offshore, they quickly captured the atoll. On February 17, troops began to land on Eniwetok, which had been pounded by American planes for three weeks. From the 14th to the 22nd, American Army and Navy planes kept up a continual attack on neighboring Japanese air bases so that enemy planes would be unable to help their comrades in the Marshalls. By the end of the month, U. S. troops had won possession of every important point in the Marshall Islands.

These captured islands were turned into a ring of forward air bases which slowly crept closer to the islands of Japan itself. But there were airfields in central China which were still closer to Japan. From these airfields the giant B-29 Super Fortresses could reach targets in Japan. But China was cut off from her allies, and her supplies had to be flown in over the mighty Himalaya mountains.

To get their transports over the mountains, the pilots had to fly against one-hundred-mile-per-hour winds and blinding snowstorms. They knew that if they were forced to land they would have almost no hope of rescue. They also had to fly at night to avoid Japanese fighter patrols. Yet, somehow, they managed to wrestle their heavily laden planes over mountain ranges as much as sixteen thousand feet high.

Meanwhile, in Europe, the Allies were pressing in toward the enemy's homeland. In September, 1943, they had crossed from Sicily to the Italian mainland. Helped as usual from the air, Allied troops managed to battle their way a considerable distance up the Italian boot. On the way they captured a valuable group of bases from which their bombers were able to reach targets in central and southeastern Europe.

But Italy was not the really important prize. The main aim of the western Allies was to land an invasion army on the French coast, push the Germans back, and then march on into Germany. To organize the invasion, some of the top Allied commanders in the Mediterranean moved back to London. General Eisenhower became commander in chief of the invasion forces and General Spaatz became overall commander of the U. S. air forces in Europe.

The Allies planned to launch the invasion early in the summer of 1944. To keep casualties down the commanders were determined to win complete mastery of the air over the invasion beaches. One way to win this mastery was to knock out Germany's aircraft plants.

Luckily for the Allied invasion plans, long-range P-51 Mustang fighters began to arrive in England early in 1944. They were able to escort bombers to almost any target in Germany, and that meant the bombers were able to start making daylight raids again on a big scale.

During one week in February, American bombers flying by day and RAF bombers flying by night severely damaged the German aircraft factories. Then, on March 4, 6, and 8, daylight bombers, escorted by Mustangs, made heavy attacks on Berlin itself. During February and March the Luftwaffe lost 800 fighters in Western Europe.

They lost 176 planes on one day alone. The Germans were able to replace many of the planes. But they could not train pilots fast enough to fill the places of those who were lost, and the Luftwaffe began to weaken rapidly.

After all the months of preparation, the Allies finally launched their invasion in the dark and windy hours before dawn on June 6. Approximately 4,000 ships were used to carry the invasion armies across the Channel while, overhead, 11,000 Allied planes formed a protective umbrella to guard the soldiers from aerial attack. Meanwhile, in those same pre-dawn hours, three divisions of airborne troops were dropped into Normandy.

During the first day of the invasion, U. S. and British planes flew more than 14,000 sorties. The long aerial offensive that had preceded the invasion had achieved its aim, and the Allies were complete masters of the air. "There was no hope," General Spaatz said later, "of making an invasion of Europe if we were going to be met by a strong German air force."

The Germans fought stubbornly to hold the Allied troops close to the beaches where they landed. Despite the tremendous hammering they took from the air, the Germans held the Allied armies back for more than a month. Then, on July 25, an American army finally broke loose and, with tanks leading the way, began to storm across the French countryside.

Every tank column was protected by fighters. To arrange co-operation, fighter pilots were put in the tanks with a radio over which they could talk to their fellow pilots in the air. General Elwood Quesada, who commanded an American Tactical Air Command, later described this arrangement as a real bonanza. "The tanks," he said, "could tell the airplanes where the targets were when the airplanes couldn't find them, and the airplanes would tell our tanks where the Germans were to avoid surprise. So it made both forces effective. The Germans would have a small contingent of tanks lying in ambush, and before they knew it, they themselves were ambushed. It was a slaughter, an outright slaughter."

Ruins and mud-filled shell holes demonstrate the havoc wreaked on Germany by Allied air power.

For several months before the invasion began, Adolf Hitler had been boasting that he possessed a secret weapon that would win the war for Germany. One week after the invasion of France, Hitler unleashed his surprise. It was a pilotless flying bomb, powered by a jet engine, and it became known as the V-1. It could fly about 150 miles at a speed of around 400 miles an hour. These flying bombs were launched against London and other targets in Britain and although more than twenty RAF squadrons were assigned to shoot them down, they did severe damage.

Shortly afterwards, Hitler unleashed another secret and much deadlier weapon—the V-2. This was also a pilotless bomb but it was powered by rockets and controlled by radio. The V-1 had made a buzzing sound in flight and when the people below heard the buzz stop, they knew the bomb was about to fall and rushed for cover. The V-2 was much more dangerous because it was silent. Shot up in an arched flight path sixty miles high at its peak, and traveling at speeds of up to 3,600 miles an hour, they would drop without warning carrying their 2,000-pound warhead.

The British were unable to shoot down the V-2's and at least a thousand of them landed in Britain. But they had been discovered too late to have much effect on the war. For by the fall of 1944 the Allied armies had captured the bases from which the rockets were launched and were pressing on toward the German frontier.

At the beginning of 1945, the British and Americans began to cut into Germany from the west while the Russians moved in from the east. On April 16, General Spaatz announced that the bombing offensive was over. There were no targets left for the bombers to destroy. A few days later, on May 7, Germany surrendered. Afterwards, the German leaders unanimously agreed that it was the Allied air power which had decided the result of the war in Europe.

The war against Japan was not yet won. But since the middle of 1944 the end had been inevitable. One of the decisive battles was that waged in the summer of 1944 for control of the Mariana

Islands of Guam, Saipan, and Tinian. The Marianas were only 1,500 miles from Japan and the Japanese leaders knew that if the islands were captured the Americans would begin massive bombing attacks on their home islands.

The Japanese made a supreme effort to smash the American attack on the Marianas. "The fate of the Empire," said Japan's prime minister, "rests on this battle." The Japanese had at least 500 land-based planes on the islands and, farther to the south, Admiral Ozawa gathered a fleet of 73 ships which included five battleships and nine aircraft carriers.

The American invasion fleet was larger than all that was left of the Japanese navy. But Ozawa's planes were lighter than the American planes and could fly farther. To take advantage of this, he planned to approach close enough to the American fleet for his planes to attack it, and yet keep far enough away so that the American planes could not reach his ships. He hoped first to destroy the American fleet and then wipe out the American invasion forces which would be left isolated on the Marianas.

But nothing went right for the Japanese. Before Ozawa's ships could get within range of the American fleet, American Grumman Hellcats had shattered the Japanese planes based on the islands. Nonetheless, Ozawa pressed on with his attack, launching his carrier-borne planes against the American fleet in four separate waves. The Hellcats shot them to pieces. Three hundred and sixty-six Japanese planes were shot down, and some American pilots were credited with as many as six kills in a single mission. To finish off the battle, submarine and air attacks destroyed a large part of Ozawa's fleet.

From this victory, the American navy turned on the Philippines. Once again, the Japanese fleet tried to block the invasion and once again it was overwhelmed. In the battle of Leyte Gulf, three Japanese battleships and four carriers were sunk, and in the air, the Japanese Zeros were shot down by the dozen.

By the summer of 1944, the Japanese air force was hopelessly outnumbered and outclassed. In desperation, the Japanese turned to one last tactic. They organized the "kamikaze" raids in which pilots deliberately crashed their planes on a target to make sure of hitting it.

These raids were very effective. During the last ten months of the war, at least five thousand Japanese airmen sacrificed their lives deliberately in the suicide attacks. The ships they damaged or sank made up one-half of America's total naval losses in the entire war.

But the kamikaze raids were the last gasp from a shattered enemy. By March, 1945, American bases had reached very close to Japan, and the American commander in charge of B-29's, General Curtis LeMay, decided to use his bombers to set Japan's cities aflame. He therefore sent them out to make low-level attacks with incendiary bombs.

The B-29's had complete mastery of the skies over Japan. They did not even need fighter escorts. From March onwards, they wiped out huge areas of sixty-nine of Japan's biggest cities and killed about a quarter of a million Japanese. But even under this terrible pounding, the Japanese showed no signs of surrender.

To defend their home islands, the Japanese had about a million soldiers and perhaps five thousand combat planes, most of which could be used as kamikazes. An invasion of Japan therefore threatened to mean severe fighting and, probably, heavy losses of American troops.

It was to avoid these losses that the United States government decided to use the most terrible weapon hitherto invented—the atom bomb. On August 6, 1945, an American pilot, Colonel Paul Tibbets, flew his B-29 over the Japanese city of Hiroshima and dropped the world's first atom bomb. That single bomb destroyed more than half of Hiroshima and killed eighty thousand people.

Three days later, another B-29 dropped a second atom bomb on the city of Nagasaki. The explosion was so violent that it shook the plane, which was 29,000 feet above the ground, "as if the B-29 were being beaten by a telephone pole."

That second atom bomb killed more than 35,000 people. The Japanese could not keep on fighting against such terrible weapons and on August 15, 1945, their government surrendered. World War II was over at last, and it may well have been their air power which had done the most to bring the Allies their victory.

CHAPTER TEN

U.S. F-105B Thunderchief fighter-bomber

Postwar

DURING the war, scores of thousands of people went up in the air for the first time. Millions more came to accept the airplane as a part of everyday life. They were ready to change their old habits and shift to traveling by air.

When the war ended, the U. S. Army was using large numbers of four-engine DC-4's and Lockheed Constellations to carry military cargoes. Less than twenty years before, Lindbergh's flight across the Atlantic had been a sensation. The DC-4's and the Constellations crossed it as casually as if they were flying across a lake. After the war, many of these planes were adapted for commercial use, to fly passengers, and for several years they were the backbone of the trans-Atlantic passenger service. Both of them, however, were powered by ordinary piston engines. Eventually they were to be replaced, on most long-distance flights, by a new kind of airplane—the jet.

The jet engine is based on the scientific principle that every action causes an equal reaction in the opposite direction. For example, if you fire a rifle, it will react to the action of the bullet by kicking back. If you release a toy balloon filled with air, the balloon will continue to travel in one direction as long as the air is rushing out through its neck in the opposite direction.

The turbojet, which is the most common type of jet engine, works on the same reaction principle. Air is sucked in through the front of the engine, is compressed, and is mixed with fuel in a combustion chamber. This mixture is set on fire and the gases, expanding as they burn, rush out through the rear of the engine with great force. It is the reaction to this force which drives the airplane forward.

On their way out, the gases strike fan blades on the turbine, thereby turning it. This turbine turns the compressor, which is also a kind of fan. It has hundreds of blades to draw in the air from in front of the plane. Thus, the action of the burned gases not only drives the airplane forward but also provides the power for drawing in more air to keep the process going.

A design for a jet engine had been patented, way back in 1930, by an Englishman named Frank Whittle. But the first jet plane to fly, in August of 1939, was a German Heinkel. When World War II broke out, both the British and the Germans worked hard to get combat jets into the air. The Germans got a fighter-bomber, the Messerschmitt Me-262, into action toward the end of 1944. Britain also produced a combat jet, the Gloster Meteor, and the U. S. flew an operational jet fighter, the Lockheed P-80, in January, 1944.

All these planes appeared too late to have much effect on the fighting. But they proved that jets

An unusual experimental plane, the Bell X-5, flies over the Southwest desert. Its wings, which could change the angle of their sweep in flight, provided much information on use of swept wings.

had important advantages over the older, piston-engine machines. They were faster and more maneuverable; they operated more efficiently at high altitudes and high speeds, and they provided a much smoother ride.

The jets also had—and still have—certain drawbacks. They need very long runways and they make a great deal of noise when taking off. But with so many advantages it was inevitable that jets would eventually replace the passenger-carrying piston planes, at least on long-distance flights.

The British were the first to put jet planes into commercial service. Actually the planes were not pure jets; they were turboprops, a kind of halfway compromise between the old piston type and the true jet. A turboprop engine works in the same way as a turbojet, but most of the force of the expanding gases is used to turn a large turbine which turns a propeller as well as the compressor.

Turboprops could not fly as fast or as high as turbojets but they could take off from a shorter runway and they used less fuel. They therefore seemed to offer the best combination of speed and economy over the short European commercial routes.

The British flew the first turboprop, the Vickers V-630 Viscount, in 1948. Four years later, the British went on to put the first true jet passenger plane into service. It was the de Havilland Comet and it flew between Britain and South Africa, Ceylon and the Far East.

Gradually, throughout the 1950's, other countries followed the British in using jets for long-distance flights. The Russians and the French each

Lockheed Constellation, once used as war transport, later blazed commercial routes to Europe.

developed their own jet airliners, and the United States produced two outstanding jet transports. One was the Boeing 707 and the other was the Douglas DC-8. Both flew at more than 30,000 feet and cruised at speeds of almost 600 miles an hour.

The introduction of such enormously powerful jets brought with it many other changes. Outside every major capital, and in many other cities also, new airports were built with runways long enough to operate the mighty jets. One of them, Idlewild (now Kennedy) International Airport, outside New York City, cost $371,000,000 to build and it handles more than 700 take-offs and landings every day. Every year, the number of people traveling by plane has continued to grow. In 1962, U. S. airlines alone carried more than 60 million passengers.

Meanwhile, even more striking advances had been made in military aircraft. During World War II, some pilots had noticed that if they flew very fast, for example in power dives, their controls ceased to work and their planes were shaken by a terrible vibration. Sometimes the planes were shaken to pieces in the air or went into uncontrollable dives from which they did not pull out.

The reason was that these planes had come up against what became known as the sound barrier. As a plane flies, it stirs up waves which travel through the air at the speed of sound. This speed is about 760 miles per hour at sea level and about 650 miles per hour above 35,000 feet. If a plane is flying below this speed, it pushes the pressure waves ahead of it, and these waves part the air, allowing the plane to go through. But when a plane itself reaches the speed of sound, it catches up with the waves and they pile up like a wall, forming a barrier in front of the plane.

If planes were to fly safely as fast as—or faster than—the speed of sound, a way had to be found for them to break through this sound barrier. But trying to break through proved extremely dangerous because the plane was liable to come to pieces. In September, 1946, this happened to an English test pilot, Geoffrey de Havilland, son of the famous designer, and he was instantly killed.

Just over a year later, in October, 1947, a twenty-five-year-old American combat veteran named Charles Yeager made another attempt to crash through the barrier. His plane, the Bell X-1, was very small. It had a long, thin nose, like a needle, and it was powered by four engines which could use up the plane's entire fuel supply in two and a half minutes. Because the X-1 could fly for only a very short time, it was carried aloft by a B-29, which launched it high in the air over California. There, Yeager became the first man to crack the sound barrier. His speed was a little over Mach 1. This way of measuring speed was named for an Austrian physicist, Dr. Ernst Mach, who had been one of the first men to experiment with the relationships between speed and sound. In his memory, the speed of sound at any given height was named Mach 1; twice the speed of sound was Mach 2, and so on.

Yeager was an experienced test pilot and he was casual about his history-making flight. "I've tried to think back to that first flight past Mach 1," he said later, "but it doesn't seem any more important than any of the others. I was at about 37,000 straight level, and it was just a matter of flying the airplane. It flew very nicely and got up to .97 on the Mach indicator, and then the meter jumped to about 1.05 as I accelerated past the shock wave that was on the nose of the airplane. I was kind of disappointed that it wasn't more of a big charge than it was."

The United States had a good reason for trying to build ever faster and better military planes. The end of World War II was followed by a worldwide struggle between communist and non-communist nations, and aircraft played a tremendously important part in it. The first big clash came in Berlin. When the war ended, Russia, France, Britain and the United States all occupied part of Germany, and all four countries took over a section of Berlin. But Berlin lay inside the Russian-occupied zone and in the summer of 1948, the Russians decided to try and force the western troops out of the city.

To do this, the Russians cut off all the overland routes which the British, Americans and French used to carry supplies into West Berlin. However, the western Allies had been guaranteed the use of three air corridors, each 20 miles wide, into Berlin. With the overland routes cut off, the Allies determined to keep West Berlin supplied from the air.

Boeing B-52F Stratofortress, showing the eight jet engines in pods underneath the wings

The operation was terribly difficult. It was successful only because it was superbly organized. Flying from bases in West Germany, British and American cargo planes reached Berlin at three-minute intervals day and night. The pilots had only one chance to land. If they did not come in right the first time, they immediately left the area so that other planes would not start stacking up behind them. The airlift was commanded by U. S. General Curtis LeMay and, as the blockade continued, it became steadily more efficient. Working furiously, the airport workers unloaded the huge transports in an average time of 49 minutes per plane. The crews had little time for more than a cup of coffee before they took off again.

In the first six weeks of the airlift, some pilots were making so many flights into Berlin that they got only four hours sleep a night. But by January, the airlift was working so smoothly that the West Berliners' food rations were greatly increased. As spring came, the weather improved and flying in and out of Berlin became a lot easier. On one day in mid-April, a total of 1,398 flights brought nearly 13,000 tons of supplies into the city.

Finally, the Russians decided that the airlift had made their blockade a failure and in May they allowed the Allies to start using the overland routes into Berlin once again.

But the communists were still probing for weak spots in the non-communists world's defenses. For their next aggressive act, they picked on the country of Korea, at the eastern tip of Asia. Before and during World War II, Korea had been occupied by the Japanese, and when the war in the Pacific ended, it was divided into two parts. The northern section was controlled by a communist government and the southern section by a non-communist one.

On June 25, 1950, the North Korean Communists invaded South Korea. Meeting in New York, the United Nations decided that its members should come to the aid of South Korea. There was little time to lose. For the South Korean army was weak and unprepared, and the North Koreans rapidly took over almost all the southern half of the country.

United States troops arrived just in time. With help from the Air Force, they began to force the North Koreans back. At first, the Air Force used fairly old planes, such as F-80 Shooting Stars and F-82 Mustangs, and B-26 and B-29 bombers which had flown in World War II. However, these planes proved good enough to smash the North Korean air force and wreck its supply lines. By November, the North Korean troops had been driven out of

Sikorsky HRS-1 helicopter evacuates casualties in Korea after bringing up replacements.

South Korea and back across their own country toward the Yalu river which formed the boundary between North Korea and Manchuria.

At this point, the Chinese Communists suddenly entered the war. Sweeping across the Yalu river, they drove the Americans back. Moreover, the Communists had begun to use Russian-built MIG-15 jet fighters which were superior to the American F-80's and F-82's.

The U. S. had to keep control of the air if the Chinese were to be kept from carrying the war back into South Korea. In mid-December, F-86A Sabre jets arrived in Korea. They were better than the F-80's but still not as good as the Russian MIGs. However, the American pilots were better fliers than the Communists, and this balanced out the inferiority of their planes.

During 1951, the Korean war bogged down into a stalemate in which neither side seemed able to push forward. The fighting on the ground became less fierce but in the air it remained intense. The Chinese Communists had 1,800 aircraft of which at least 1,000 were jets. But they were held back by the F-86F Sabre jets which began to reach Korea in 1953. These Sabres proved far superior to the MIGs. In May, 1953, for example, Sabre pilots claimed to have shot down 53 MIGs and only one Sabre was lost. In June, U. S. pilots claimed to have shot down 75 MIGs but lost not a single Sabre. Still, the U. N. and the Communist negotiators kept trying and failing to reach an agreement on how to end the war. To help persuade the Communists that they should agree on terms, U. S. bombers carried out two tremendously important attacks.

The first, on May 13, was carried out by 59 Thunderjets against a huge irrigation dam in North Korea. The dam held up waters which were stored in reservoirs ready to irrigate North Korea's rice fields. On the night after the attack, the stored-up waters broke through the damaged dam and flooded the countryside for miles around.

Three days later, 90 F-84's caused another flood by blasting open another North Korean dam. Perhaps it was these two attacks which made the Communists decide to agree on peace terms. Whatever the reason, an armistice was signed on July 27, 1953, and the Korean war was ended.

100

The U. N. forces had not defeated the Communist armies but they had achieved their two main objectives. They had halted the Communists' attack and they had kept South Korea independent. As in World War II, U. S. air power had played a decisive part. "Without the support . . . of your air and naval forces," the North Korean General Nam Il admitted, "your ground forces would have long ago been driven out of the Korean peninsula."

During the Korean war, a new kind of flying craft, the helicopter, was used in larger numbers than ever before. Unlike airplanes, a helicopter does not have any wings. Nor does it have a propeller. Instead, the engine turns a rotor blade situated on top of the fuselage. This rotor, which turns horizontally, takes the place of both wings and propeller. For the helicopter is kept aloft by the "lift" provided by the air which is stirred up by the revolving rotor.

During the 1930's, designers, trying to produce a workable helicopter, were baffled by one problem: the rotor blade, turning in one direction, throws the machine over onto one side. But in 1939, a Russian-born American named Igor Sikorsky came up with a solution. He mounted a small, vertical propeller on the left side of his helicopter's body, and so produced a balancing counter-effect.

Because the rotor turns horizontally, a helicopter can rise almost straight upwards. To fly forward, the machine must be dipped so that the rotor bites into the air at an angle off the horizontal. But though it might seem clumsy, the helicopter has several advantages over an ordinary airplane. It can fly and land at slow speeds. It can hover, almost motionless, in the air for indefinite periods. It can be maneuvered with great precision. And it can land in an open space the size of a tennis court.

Helicopters have proved to be extremely useful in peace and in war. They are used, among other purposes, to transport passengers out from city centers to airports and so avoid traffic delays, to carry mail and direct traffic, and to rescue people caught in floods or trapped on mountainsides or other places accessible only from the air.

In the Korean war, helicopters were used largely to pick up wounded soldiers and fly them back to

The USAF A-11 jet, the existence of which was announced by President Johnson February 29, 1964.

hospitals. But helicopters have also served as aggressive weapons. They are especially useful for transporting large numbers of soldiers in a hurry to a particular spot. Sikorsky himself developed the S-56 which could carry 36 fully armed Marines, and the Russians have a helicopter which can carry either 180 soldiers or a whole prefabricated house.

In the past few years, many private individuals have bought helicopters. Many more have bought airplanes. Sometimes these privately owned aircraft are used for pleasure but most of them are for business. Big companies have planes of their own to fly executives around the country. Out West, ranchers may inspect their cattle from low-flying planes and surveyors take to the air to cover watery land.

Meanwhile, throughout the 1950's, the armed services were producing a succession of new airplanes which were able to perform amazing feats. One plane, the Lockheed F104 Starfighter, could fly straight up, faster than sound. The Navy's Convair XFY-1 could make a vertical take-off and also a vertical landing, settling down on the four points in its tail. And another Navy plane, the F80-1 Crusader, proved able to fly at 1,015 miles per hour, a remarkable performance for a plane able to land on an aircraft carrier.

However, these faster planes obviously needed more space to land and so bigger carriers had to be built to accommodate them. One of these new ships, the U. S. S. *Enterprise,* was the world's first nuclear-powered carrier and it has a flight deck which covers four and a half acres.

Some of the new planes were given a curious looking "coke-bottle," or "wasp-waist," shaped body. This design was thought up by an American named Richard Whitcomb. Through experiments with wind tunnels, he worked out the best possible shape for a supersonic plane which had to force its way through immensely powerful shock waves. Whitcomb pinched in the fuselage at the point where the wings join it and he added bulges to the rear of the fuselage. When these planes were tested, Whitcomb was proved right. They suffered less vibration than other models and slipped easily through the sound barrier.

Some of these planes flew at fantastic speeds. Back in 1947, Charles Yeager had set up a new speed record by flying just over Mach 1. This remained a record until August, 1951, when a Navy Douglas Skyrocket reached Mach 1.89. Just over two years later, Yeager recaptured the record by flying at Mach 2.5, or 1,650 miles per hour. But in June, 1962, a North American X-15 rocket plane was taken up to a height of 250,000 feet—about 47 miles—and there flew at the extraordinary speed of Mach 6.04, or 4,093 miles per hour.

The planes which kept breaking speed records were small, fighter-type planes. But the U. S. also maintained a large fleet of bombers. For many years after World War II ended, the Communists possessed much stronger armies than the western Allies. The U. S. therefore organized a Strategic Air Command made up of planes which, if necessary, could reply to any attack by launching nuclear bombs against the aggressor nation. Because its purpose was to discourage—or deter— any enemy from starting a war, the SAC bomber force became known as the deterrent.

In the early 1950's, SAC's most powerful bomber was the huge six-engined Convair B-36. From one or another of a series of air bases set up around the world, the B-36's could reach any target on earth.

Striving for an ever more efficient deterrent, the Air Force kept building better bombers. In 1951, the fleet of B-36's began to be replaced by six-engine jet B-47's which, despite their size, carried a crew of only three men. In the mid-1950's, B-52's began to come off the assembly lines.

They were huge eight-engine jets which could fly at over 600 miles per hour while carrying a formidable variety of weapons. Then, in 1956, the supersonic delta-winged B-58 made its first flight. Six years later, in March, 1962, the world was given a glimpse of this plane's amazing performance when a B-58 flew from Los Angeles to New York and back in four hours and 42 minutes.

These bombers were all manned by crews. But both the U. S. and Russia were also developing unmanned missiles which could be fired as far as a plane could fly. These missiles were rockets with a bomb (or warhead) attached, and they worked on the same general principle as the V-2 which the Germans had used during World War II.

The Russians started to concentrate on building extremely powerful rockets before the U. S., and they were therefore able to build up a big lead in the race to produce the most deadly and efficient missiles. In September, 1956, a U. S. Army rocket team managed to fire a Redstone rocket for a distance of 3,000 miles. But in October, 1957, the Russians easily beat this accomplishment. They succeeded in firing a rocket which traveled at 18,000 miles per hour, fast enough to overcome the gravitational pull of the earth.

This rocket carried a hollow globe which was made of aluminum and other metals and had a diameter of just under 23 inches. It went into orbit around the earth, like a tiny moon, and thus became the first man-made space satellite.

Obviously, any booster that could put a satellite into orbit could also be used to fire missiles several thousand miles. Presumably, therefore, the Russians were able to fire rockets far enough to reach the United States. Spurred on by the Russian success, the U. S. rapidly quickened its efforts to develop a booster of equal power.

By the fall of 1959, the U. S. Air Force had developed the Atlas intercontinental ballistic missile (ICBM). It was given this name because it could be fired thousands of miles, from one continent to another. Then, on April 12, 1961, the Russian Yuri Gagarin became the first man to be shot into space and sent into orbit around the

Mass of private planes at Lockhaven, Pa., typifies enormous increase in use of small planes.

earth. But by February, 1962, the U. S. copied
this tremendous achievement by sending Lieutenant Colonel John Glenn up into space and three
times around the earth.

To some people, it seemed that the development
of rocket-powered ICBM's had made manned
bombers and fighters obsolete. In theory, any
country which possessed ICBM's could start a war
by firing them across the world. The other country,
also in theory, would send up anti-missile missiles
to explode the attacking ICBM's in the air. At the
same time, it would also retaliate by firing its own
ICBM's against the enemy.

This stage has not yet been reached. No country,
as far as is known, yet possesses a missile system
which can be relied on to intercept all incoming
missiles. And the U. S. is still keeping its SAC
bombers ready to reply to any nuclear attack at
a moment's notice.

However, the flights into space have undoubtedly opened a new and enormously exciting stage in
man's exploration of the skies. More powerful
boosters will certainly be built, able to send much
larger and heavier loads up into space. Before too
long, vehicles may be launched able to refuel in
space and navigate without trouble in and out of
the earth's atmosphere. Probably these space vehicles will reach the moon and perhaps other,
more distant worlds also.

The pace of man's inventions has quickened
enormously in this century. Man lived on earth
for hundreds of thousands of years before he
learned to fly. But in a mere sixty years, he has
advanced from the Wrights' flying machine to the
satellites which have spun him in orbit around
the earth. No one can foretell what new and amazing discoveries the next sixty years may bring.

"Our efforts today," as Lieutenant Colonel
Glenn told the United States Congress, "and what
we've done so far are but small building blocks on
a very huge pyramid to come . . . Knowledge be-
gets knowledge. The more I see, the more impressed I am not with how much we know but with
how tremendous the areas are that are yet un-
explored."

INDEX

Famous Airplanes: POST-WORLD WAR II

CONVAIR B-36D 1949

BOEING B-47 STRATOJET 1947

PIPER AZTEC 1960

BOEING 707-320B 1962